Preacher
"A Man Sent From God"

The Life And Times Of Rev. Earl W. Freeland

by Bud Key Sr.

Revised and Updated November 2014

Proceeds from sales of **Preacher "A Man Sent From God"** to benefit the Earl W. Freeland Scholarship at Alliance Christian Academy in Portsmouth, VA.

ACKNOWLEDGMENTS

This updated and revised edition of **Preacher** *"A Man Sent From God"* has been a true labor of love for the author. It has rekindled fond memories of his pastor and friend. He is indebted to those who encouraged him and is confident their reward will be in seeing young men and women realize their dream of a college education become a reality partly through the Earl W. Freeland Scholarship.

Words cannot express his love and appreciation to Bud Key, Jr., his patient and understanding editor who was always there to keep the author headed in the right direction. Sons are like that.

And as always there is Pris, the author's wife and best friend. She inspired the book as she has his life.

Dedicated to Pris, Jack, Bailey and Canaan

A NEW FOREWORD

Earl Walter Freeland, Sr., was my pastor from 1982 to '87 and a treasured friend until his death in August 2006. Preacher was, unquestionably, one of the most fascinating and God-loving men I ever met. I was privileged to spend many hours with him, oftentimes on his front porch or hanging around the baseball field in front of his home. This book, first published in early 2000, is the story of a man sent from God to make this world a better place. It is also an invitation to kick back and share a remarkable journey as seen through Preacher's eyes as well as those of his wife, Freda, his children and friends. It includes a mixture of laughter, tears, ups and downs, and ultimately God's goodness for those who faithfully honor and proclaim His glorious name.

Raised by parents who had little or no time for love, Preacher Freeland grew up in a small West Virginia mountain town, drifted aimlessly as a teenager, and wound up — like nearly everyone else in his community — working as a coal miner. He married and was living a life of sin. After accepting Jesus Christ as his personal Savior, he attended a Christian & Missionary Alliance college and became an ordained minister. He then pastored three churches in Pennsylvania before coming to Portsmouth, VA, in 1959 to fulfill God's call. He built a church and a Christian school and served as pastor of the Portsmouth Christian & Missionary Alliance until his retirement in 1987. That is a clinical look at his life. Dull stuff? Nothing could be further from the truth. At every step along the way, we peel off another layer of this man's willingness to let God work through him. From a young man whose gambling habit was so ingrained he would bet on which fence post a bird would land on to a pastor who would raise up a church of nearly 500 members, you will witness God's awesome power and Preacher's unyielding faith.

When I started writing **Preacher *"A Man Sent From God"*** some 15 years ago, I experienced serious doubts. Could I tell the story? Would anyone want to read it? I remember sharing my concerns with my son who, without hesitation, answered: "Dad, a hundred years from now somebody might find a copy and read it. Then they will know what it was like to be a real preacher of God's word." When I had finished and all the copies were sold, never in a million years did I think someday I would pick up where the book left off and have it republished. Or that, as my son tried to explain to me, folks would be able to read it electronically on their smart phones and tablets. God certainly does work in mysterious ways, doesn't He? Enjoy yourself and may God richly bless you.

Bud Key, Sr.
August 2014

PROLOGUE

It was a lazy fall afternoon and the leaves from all those trees were just starting to fall. June was sitting on the front porch of his home enjoying the million or so squirrels, birds, cats, dogs and other unidentified animals as they paraded by. Of course, it wasn't his home by legal definition but the parsonage of the Portsmouth (VA) Christian & Missionary Alliance Church. And the only person this side of West Virginia who knew him by "June" was his wife, Freda. To the multitude of people in Portsmouth who knew and loved him he was Pastor Earl Freeland or most often simply "Preacher." And this afternoon Preacher was doing what he'd done as often as possible since 1963, when the church built the house on the back side of the church property. He was looking over the 10 or so acres of church property and the magnificent church the Lord had blessed the congregation with. Preacher closed his eyes and leaned back. It was impossible to tell whether he was dreaming or just remembering.

He had been the pastor at three churches in Pennsylvania before God told him to come to Portsmouth and build a church. Seemed like every time he had gotten comfortable there was that small voice and it usually meant one of three things — move, renovate or build. This afternoon Preacher was confident in his own mind those days were over. He was certain he was in God's will in Portsmouth. The church and fellowship hall were a perfect fit for the congregation. All was well. He would serve the church as long as God wanted him there. And then he would retire. A serene nap was interrupted by the barking of a hound chasing a squirrel, causing him to sit up and again look over the property. Seemed to him it was an awful lot of land for just a church, fellowship hall and ranch home. And then, the tap on his shoulder. As he looked across the property he heard something. Not the chirping of birds or the bark of that ole' hound dog. No, it was the sound of a bouncing basketball. Here we go again, he thought. Time to build a school.

ORIGINAL INTRODUCTION
"A Man Sent From God"...

Intriguing words of God used to introduce the writer of the fourth gospel are simple but profound. They are concise, clear and compelling:

As found in **John 1:7-8**, *"There was a man sent by God..., whose name was John. The same came for a witness to bear witness of the Light, that all men through Him might believe."* Such words were highly complimentary, as they express John's grandest purpose.

This book is a fascinating adventure of another "man sent from God."

In God's providence, I met him about two years after I trusted in Jesus Christ as my Savior and Lord. I was deeply troubled by some doctrinal teaching that encouraged me to seek an experience that would eradicate my "old sinful, selfish Adamic nature." I earnestly sought for such as experience, but became disillusioned by the inconsistencies of those who taught it.

I prayed and sought God's guidance. Shortly after, a friend invited me to hear their new pastor. I listened carefully to his preaching. He loved to preach the word; proclaim the transforming power of the Gospel; and exalt Jesus Christ as the one trustworthy Lord of the Christian lifestyle.

His life was marked with integrity of character, spiritual authenticity and tenderhearted compassion. It was quickly obvious that Jesus Christ had taught him how to love God; how to love his family; how to love people; and how to love life. There was a contagious joy, a generous spirit, and an attitude of hope that impacted the atmosphere when he was present.

There was a man sent from God whose name was... Earl.

Little did I understand how well he was modeling ministry for me as I listened to him preach, heard him pray, watched him tease children, and play sports with young people. In him I saw the sobering reverence of God's call and the wisdom of healthy humor. He was unpretentious about himself but keenly aware he was Christ's ambassador in a world of hurting lost people.

There was a man sent from God whose name was... Earl.

Please understand I never call him by his first name. He was first Rev. Freeland, or as he preferred, Pastor Freeland, but since August 28, 1953, I have called him "Dad Freeland" or just "Dad." His lovely daughter, Barbara, and I were united in marriage by Dad in the Bradford Alliance Church in Pennsylvania.

So, for nearly 43 years, I have known him intimately. We have shared as fellow laborers in the Gospel in the Christian & Missionary Alliance Church for 38 years. He has been my treasured "mentor" in so many ways. His mature insight often prevented serious mistakes in my ministry and at times offered wisdom to learn from tough experiences. When Barbara and I have needed encouragement, prayer, spiritual insight, or practical help... there was a man sent from God who name was...

For the significant number of people who needed God's timely intervention and who can testify to God's gracious providence, I echo their grateful affirmation.

There was a man sent from God whose name was... Preacher Freeland.

— **Rev. James E. Vandervort**
May 2000

P.S. As you read this book, you will understand it requires a postscript from all of us that will be highlighted in capital letters in eternity. It will read like this... There was a woman sent from God to greatly influence Earl's life and ours... her name was Freda.

EDITOR'S INTRODUCTION

Genesis 1:1: *"In the beginning..."* As a reporter, editor and publisher for nearly 30 years, I've learned a few writing tips in my career. One of the most important is to always include a backstory. I remember very little about the sequence, effort and circumstances that led up to the original printing of **Preacher "A Man Sent From God."** Although my dad insists I edited the first version for him, I have serious doubts I gave it much more than a cursory glance. It was his project, not mine.

A signed, first edition copy of the book has sat collecting dust on my bookshelf for the past 14 or so years. Not entirely out-of-sight, but certainly out-of-mind... until a couple months ago. Through an amazing series of events you'll read about later, he asked me — in a technical sense — what it would take to reprint the book. I've worked on several of dad's "projects" before and knew instinctively where he was headed. No way was I going to take the bait, again. So I gave him a stock answer. Take the original camera-ready copy to a local printer, pay them several thousand dollars, and, although not verbalized but implied, leave me out of it. Case closed...

Until late that night. My wife and kids had gone to bed and, as I do often, I sat reclined in my easy chair watching *SportsCenter* on ESPN. Having already seen the same highlights several times, and for no other apparent reason, I picked up the **Preacher** book and read the first few pages. And cringed. While mildly entertaining, all I could really see were the grammatical errors, spelling typos and run-on sentences. Why, I asked myself, would dad want to have it reprinted? And who would want to read it now after so many years had passed? It had been a nice gesture on his part back then; a self-published book about his local preacher. Nothing more. So I went to bed...

And woke up 30 minutes later. By sunrise, I had read the entire book. Really read it this time. Tears? I cried a boatload. Conviction? I asked God to forgive me of every sin in my life going back to the time I punched Sonny Meeks in kindergarten. Smiles? A lot of those, too. I realized **Preacher "A Man Sent From God"** — literary warts and all — did deserve another go-round. And with God's guidance, I would help dad make it happen. Oh, sure. I would still complain and grumble about it. That's always been my curious way of showing dad how much I love him.

So about this new edition of **Preacher**. First, I have tried to clean-up and correct the human errors (misspelled words, etc.) that appeared in the original. I have also attempted to make sense of several timeline inaccuracies. Moreover, I have hopefully "spruced" up the writing style a bit. But this book remains 100 percent my dad's work and his intent to tell the story of Pastor Freeland's life remains intact. Second, the book is now complete with the addition of several new chapters —

ones that pick up the story where it left off in early 2000. And lastly, it has been made available not only in print but also in various e-book formats.

One last question must be addressed. Who will want to read it? I admit, I wrestled with that one for quite a while. On the surface, as I alluded to, **Preacher** would appear to be localized and geared toward those who knew Rev. Freeland. I no longer believe this to be true or accurate. This book is a fascinating account of a "man sent from God" that transcends the geographical boundaries of Portsmouth, VA. Because, in reality, it is the story of what Jesus Christ can accomplish in anybody's life if they choose to believe in Him. That opens a really big door. For Christians, I believe this book will strengthen your faith and remind you of the urgency to share the Gospel of Christ. For those of you going into or already studying for the ministry, this book can be a source of advice and inspiration. For current pastors, Sunday School teachers and youth leaders, you might just pick up a sermon or lesson idea. Finally, and most importantly, **Preacher *"A Man Sent From God"*** is compassionately written for the sinner in all of us. For it is those whom Pastor Freeland showed his love to most.

Lord, the fleece has now been laid at Your feet.

— **Bud Key, Jr.**
August 2014

Chapter 1

Look Out World, Here I Come

"Let the little children come to me, and do not hinder them, for the kingdom of God belongs to such as these." **Mark 10:14 (NIV)**

Autumn is God's most colorful season... a canopy of flaming reds, crisp oranges, harvested yellows and earth-toned browns. I have marveled at the palette He chose for over 80 years now, always believing it is one of His many ways of showing us just how beautiful Heaven will be. The fall months. Or more precisely, as a launching point for this book, October 4, 1981. So many years ago. And while it is true I now sometimes forget where I laid my keys or who won the ball game I watched on television the night before, that particular date remains a sweet memory. For it was the evening I heard the personal testimony of a man sent from God.

The night was cool and lazy... comfortable in a flannel shirt sort of way. Not that anyone would have seriously considered wearing brushed plaid. Back then, attending a Sunday evening service still called for a degree of fashion decorum. For the men of the church, that meant wearing a suit or sports jacket (sans the necktie if you were a little younger) or, if feeling a bit rebellious, at least nicely-starched Khakis and an Izod sweater. The idea of showing up in your best "holy" jeans hadn't made its way into sanctuaries in the South just yet. Neither had pastors dressed up like Don Ho in Hawaiian shirts and flip-flops. The ladies that evening were dressed conservatively, too, with the only noticeable nod to the trends of the day being their ginormous hairstyles. Even the teenagers — most who were understandably eager for the service to end so they could get to the local Shoney's Restaurant before the Baptists and Pentecostals down the road got all the good seats — showed reasonable restraint in their wardrobe choices. It was a small price to pay for the chance to spend an hour or so holding hands in one of the back pews. With text messaging, Facebook and on-line dating websites still years away, attending a Sunday evening church service was still one of the best places to catch the eye of a pretty girl or an eligible young man.

As most every Sunday evening since June 1959, Preacher Earl Freeland was on the stage of the Portsmouth (VA) Christian & Missionary Alliance Church preparing to deliver the sermon the Lord had laid on his heart — a message he had prayed over, studied and jotted down on not much more than a scrap piece of paper. But first he took time to enjoy the singing. Preacher Freeland often thanked the Lord for blessing his church with what was arguably the best music program in the Tidewater area. Or the entire world, in his eyes. In fact, several church members and groups — among them Chuck Conti, Delores Taylor and the Alliance Trio — had recorded gospel albums. To this day, I still sometimes sneak out to my workshop

[12]

and listen to their cassette tapes. Or at least to the ones that haven't been "eaten" by the old stereo player I picked up at a yard sale years ago.

With the music portion of the service complete, Preacher Freeland rose from his chair on stage, straightened out his pants legs, and strolled to the pulpit. It was his most favorite place to be, and he commanded it with the meekness of a lamb and the protectiveness of a mountain lion. Like so many times before, Preacher sensed the Holy Spirit permeating the sanctuary that evening. "Lord, we sense your presence in an unusual way tonight. We believe Thou has come to speak to our hearts. Help thy servant to obey Thee in all Thou hast said. And I pray there shall be listening ears and hearts that need that which You have said. I pray this in the name of Jesus. Amen." After that heartfelt prayer, he opened his Bible and read the first 14 verses from **Psalm 107**: *"Oh give thanks unto the Lord for He is good... He brought them out of darkness and the shadow of death and broken their bands of sunder."*

With the scripture reading complete, Preacher Freeland began what certainly promised to be another one of his surprisingly simple yet deeply profound sermons from a man who could literally preach the paint off a barn. And then he stopped just as abruptly as he had begun. I doubt there was a believer or non-believer, saint or sinner, who didn't feel the warm touch of the Holy Spirit enter the building during those precious few moments. And then, almost apologetically, Preacher spoke: "I must do something that I do not do very often, and have not done, and I think my wife can testify to that, very often through the years of my ministry. While I was sitting on the platform, God spoke to my heart. I had another message prepared out of this Psalm tonight. But God has instructed me and I want to share with you my testimony. I believe there is someone here who especially needs to hear what God has done in my life — maybe to encourage you to trust Him a little bit more. I was born in a little town in West Virginia named..."

His father, Earl Marquis Freeland, was from Monumental, WV. Although informally trained as a mechanic, his dad was determined to find his fame and glory — and fill his pockets with a few extra coins — as a minstrel actor in a Vaudeville show. Preacher's mom, Mahalia, meanwhile banged out saloon songs on the piano in a competing traveling act. Since both groups played the same small mountain towns, it was inevitable the two would meet. It was love at first sight and Earl and Mahalia quickly married and settled in the tiny railroad town of Cunningham, WV. The couple was still seeking their "big" entertainment break when on April 10, 1916, Earl Walter Freeland, Preacher, was born. His parents thought he was just about the prettiest 10-pound baby boy they had ever seen. Many years later, Preacher would admit he couldn't remember if somebody had told him that or if he'd simply made it up.

Preacher's only real memory of his parents' Vaudeville act occurred at about the age of five when his dad gave him a small part in their act. He would run onto the makeshift stage with a bundle of newspapers yelling, "The woods are full of them, the woods are full of them." At some point his dad would then ask, "Full of what?" Standing as tall and as proud as possible, Preacher would yell in his best theatrical voice, "Full of trees."

Remembering even further back, Preacher recalled first learning about the principles of sharing at the age of two or so. It came with the birth of his sister, Florence May (Babe). Like any good big brother, Preacher took Babe under his wing and actually looked forward to the times when his mother was busy and he would have to look after his baby sister. More times than not, he would take her bottle, crawl under the bed, and drink the milk. "You talk about an undernourished baby girl." Preacher also remembered becoming a master mud pie maker at an early age. He and his hooligan friends — none older than four or five — would spend hours making the mud pies and then climb on top of a shed or up a tree. "Our favorite targets were the straw hats on the men who walked by. There wasn't a clean straw hat in the county."

For the first few years of his life, Preacher had the curliest and most resplendent red hair in the county. But this unruly mop of mane piled on top of a cherubim face belied the fact that he was, as anyone who lived within 10 country miles of him would agree, plain "snake" mean. Still, that red hair and angelic face caught the attention of a traveling photographer who, after getting permission from Mahalia, took Preacher's picture. He then entered it into a beauty contest and, wouldn't you know it, won first place. Preacher's red locks might have been cute to most folks, but not to his Uncle Dick. One day, while babysitting with Preacher, Uncle Dick took him to the local barber shop and had his head shaved as bald as a cue ball. And then something strange happened. The hair started growing back brown and as straight as Cupid's arrow. "Stayed that way. With my background in Vaudeville, if my hair had stayed red and curly, I might have become quite famous in West Virginia."

With two small children to raise, Preacher's parents reluctantly decided there wasn't enough money in show business to pay the bills. As luck would have it, his dad heard about a job in Texas working on an oil rig. "I guess he thought he was going to become an oil baron or something, 'cause he loaded us up when I was about five and we headed for Texas." That was a grand adventure for a boy Preacher's age. Soon after they arrived, his dad found work as a tool maker on an oil rig named the One-O-One. He later became an oil well digger on the ranch, one of the first such operations in Texas.

So the early 1920s found the Freeland clan living in a company-owned shack. There was a large field of broom sage between the "house" and oil rig, and Preacher spent many hours playing in the front yard or just sitting on the porch. Although his dad walked a path through the broom sage to work every day, Preacher had never ventured into the tall, bushy beard grass. That all changed the day his mother decided to make a big plate of fudge. Thinking it would be a big treat and even bigger surprise for her husband, Mahalia wrapped up the fudge and told Preacher to take it to his dad at work. Life was pretty boring, and Preacher jumped at the chance to see the oil rig up close. The journey started out splendidly until Preacher realized he had somehow left the path and was lost in a huge field where all he could see was broom sage taller than he was. "I can't remember how long I wondered around in that dumb broom sage, but I do remember I had no idea where the oil rig or our house was. I started yelling and crying. I must have had good lungs because someone finally came and rescued me." But there was still one problem. When he was finally found, all Preacher had in his hands was an empty fudge plate. "I must have lost that fudge while I was wondering around. Of course, a piece or two might have been lost in my mouth."

Although life in Texas was mundane at best, Preacher made the most of the couple of years he spent there. It was during this time, in fact, that he "owned" the only official pet he ever had. "I had me a great big rabbit that I kept in a box in the house. I think dad caught him in a trap. One night my rabbit was making so much noise thumping his tail against the box that my mom couldn't stand it. She let that thing out of the box and I never saw it again. Boy, was I disgusted. That rabbit was really something special, really fast. I don't remember giving my rabbit an official name. I think I just called him Jack."

It only took a couple of years for Preacher's dad to figure out he probably wouldn't be the next Anthony F. Lucas. So his parents decided it would probably be best to move back home to West Virginia. Although he was in Texas for only a short while, Preacher often thought about his experiences there. Especially the day he spent alone and afraid in the broom sage. It was the first time in his life that he had felt totally lost. And though his parents had never taken him to Sunday School or church, he decided God must have let him be found for some untold reason.

When they arrived back in West Virginia, the Freelands were plum broke and could not afford to pay for a place to live. With nowhere else to turn, they moved in with his dad's father in Barrickville. Preacher's grandfather was a blacksmith and the days and nights spent in his home were happy ones. Not too long after returning, Preacher's dad found work in the nearby Number 7 coal mine. It was time to start a new chapter in Preacher's life.

By now Preacher was old enough for school, a small one-room building that housed grades first through fifth. It didn't take long for him to realize recess was his best and favorite subject. Preacher loved the big merry-go-round that was in the school yard. It consisted of a wooden board laid on a tree trunk with a rusty bolt running through it. So much for expensive playground equipment. One day the boys got carried away playing on it and Preacher wound up with a deep cut on his left index finger. The scar never went away, and the story of how he got it took on a life of its own over the years.

One of Preacher's favorite hobbies as a youngster was catching june bugs — small beetles less than in inch long that got their name because they would emerge in large quantities early each summer. Often Preacher would put his prized collection in a fruit jar and carry them to school. Some of the other kids would sometimes do the same, but to Preacher, catching these winged, hard-cased insects was a passion. So much so that he picked up the nickname "June Bug." It was a moniker his friends in West Virginia would call him by for the rest of his life.

Just before his 13th birthday, Preacher started attending "regular" school in Barrickville. Miraculously he had made it to the sixth grade and the students had a classroom all to themselves. It was about this time his parents finally were able to move to their own house at the coal mine camp. His dad, who had started out working in the mine as a blacksmith, had become a master mechanic. The coal mine was flourishing and had become the largest coal-producing outlet in West Virginia unearthing nearly 3,500 tons per day. The mine employed 1,700 men and if you lived anywhere near the area, you probably worked there. The entrance to the mine was located in a valley flanked by two large hills. It didn't take Preacher long to find out if you lived on one of the hills, you were the bitter enemy of anyone living on the other. There were daily scraps between the boys on the two mountains, with everything from BB guns to rocks and fists employed as weapons. "I suppose if we had more powerful guns we would have used them, too." One day Preacher and a boy from the other hill squared off. "We fought and we fought, I mean to tell you, 'til we were both so tired we couldn't stand. There was a log there, so we decided to call a truce. We sat down, me on one end and him on the other, 'til we got rested. Then we got up and started all over again. I got a bloody nose and had a black eye, but we sealed something that day and became close friends. Guess we knocked some sense into each other."

Not all of his time was spent waging war. Preacher had never shared a single common interest with his dad up to that point in his life. Baseball changed that. His dad had a decent fastball and pitched on a community team against other local squads. Preacher would go to the games and watch with pride as his dad played. And occasionally, father and son would play catch in the backyard after school or work. It was Preacher's fondest memory of his dad from those early years and one he hid away in his heart for the rest of his life. Preacher also recalled one of the funniest things he had ever witnessed at the ballpark. His dad, never a great hitter, had blasted a sure triple to the outfield gap and, after rounding second base, flew into third base with a head-first slide. Except it wasn't exactly third base. Instead, it was where a cow had visited between innings. His dad ended up ripping his shirt and when they got home his mom declared he smelled like a pole cat and would have to sleep outside until the stench was gone.

A nice memory, for sure. But one of the few. Now a young teenager, Preacher was painfully aware something was missing from his life. Love. He could not remember a single time sitting in his mom or dad's lap, and he longed to be hugged just one time. There was never any outward show of affection in his home. Instead, and he hated to admit it, he believed his parents loved the bottle as much or more than him or his sister. Both had become heavy drinkers and many afternoons his mom would give him money to go purchase moonshine whiskey from Black Handers. "I can still close my eyes and see the store that was really a front for selling illegal whiskey." Preacher would give the shop owner the money and receive a paper bag containing a quart jar filled with the most awful smelling (and tasting) stuff imaginable. His mother never shared this stash with Preacher's dad, instead keeping it for herself. And though she drank constantly, Preacher said surprisingly he never saw her when she appeared to be drunk.

"During this time I never went to church or Bible School. I had no exposure to the church or the Lord. Religion was not even a remote part of my life." Preacher had been exposed to sin for as long as he could remember and now it was starting to slowly creep into his own personal life. It was on this note that he began his high school years.

Chapter 2

Who Said High School Was All Homework?

"For sin shall not be your master, because you are not under law, but under grace." **Romans 6:14 (NIV)**

It would be real stretch to say Preacher was a good student in high school. Okay, it would be a lie. "I wasn't interested in anything but recess and the end of the day." And sports. A good athlete, he would end up playing baseball, football and basketball all four years at Barrickville High School. And though he never worked a real job during those four years, he knew once his high school career was over he would end up in the coal mine like almost everybody else anyway. Might as well enjoy what little "life" he had left before reporting underground, he figured.

As a freshman, Preacher tried out for football and made the varsity team. For the first time in his life he felt like he really belonged to something. During his four years, Preacher played halfback on offense (which he loved) and defensive end (which he hated). He had always dreamed of scoring the winning touchdown in a big game. But ironically, it was on defense that he first tasted the thrill of being the school hero for a day. They were playing their rival high school from nearby Fairmont whose star fullback was as big and strong as a mule. And just about as stubborn to tackle. By now Preacher had grown to a height of about 5-foot-10, give or take a few inches, and weighed 130 pounds soaking wet... with his shoes on... and rocks in his pockets. It was the same weight he would carry throughout high school. Early in the game, Preacher saw this fullback bulldozing his way with what seemed like 50 blockers in front of him. They collided head-on and you could have put butter and syrup on Preacher and used him for a pancake. Late in the game, Preacher made up for it when the same fullback rumbled around the other end for what was sure to be the winning touchdown. Dodging blockers and sprinting all the way across the field, Preacher got the perfect angle and somehow made the game-saving tackle. Years later after becoming a Christian and reading the Bible, the image of that Fairmont High fullback always came back to him whenever he taught Sunday School or preached a sermon about David and Goliath.

Later in the season, Preacher tackled another runner and somehow managed to get his finger caught in the ear hole of the player's helmet. Although he broke his finger, the incident did have a silver lining. "I got out of typing class for two whole weeks." Preacher's football career at Barrickville High is best summed up by his own submission: "I wasn't afraid of the devil himself. I took my beatings because I was so small, but I had a lot of guts. I never gave up." That same tenacity followed Preacher throughout his ministry. Heaven will be full of many men and women who Preacher refused to give up on.

After football practice, Preacher would walk two miles home for supper and then walk straight back to town and "hang out" for the evening. His parents didn't care and never once asked him anything about his day or where he was headed. Preacher decided early on that if he ever did have children, they would never lack for love. Once back to Barrickville, he would look up a couple of buddies and try to figure out what they were going to do that evening. "There wasn't much to do. We spent most of the time at the little drug store or lying on the grass in front of the Methodist Church." It was in front of that church the he and brothers Ralph and Omer Michaels planned the infamous "Chamber Pot" caper. That night, armed with an old-fashioned porcelain piss pot, Preacher climbed the flag pole in front of the school and unceremoniously attached it to the very top. The school's principal, a little short guy with a deformed arm and a terrible temper, was absolutely furious the next morning. Known for the rubber hose he used for punishment, the principal never did identify the culprits and the pot stayed on the flag pole for a couple of weeks until someone finally climbed up and got it down.

By the end of the football season, Mr. Hamilton — who served as the football, basketball and baseball coach — had become Preacher's first real male role model. He had taken a liking to Preacher as well, and invited him to come out for basketball. With nothing better to do, Preacher decided to give it a shot. He immediately fell in love with the sport and spent hours improving his skills. In no time Preacher was the best under-handed foul shooter in the conference.

During his junior year one of the basketball players raided a moonshine still and stole several quarts of "white lightning" whiskey which Preacher and five other teammates took to a covered bridge. "I can still close my eyes and see that dumb night, drinking whiskey out of quart fruit jars." The next day, a player got into an argument with Coach Hamilton and was kicked off the team. Preacher and the others he had been drinking with went to see Coach Hamilton to see if they could change his mind, but when he saw the condition they were in, he threw them off the team, as well. Preacher figured his athletic career at Barrickville was over. But a few days later, all six of the basketball players were reinstated. "I guess he had to put us back on since he didn't have enough players left to field a team."

Preacher loved playing football and basketball, but baseball was his real passion. His varsity career got off to a shaky start, however, on the very first day of practice. Coach Hamilton put Preacher in the outfield, and when the first fly ball was hit his direction, he circled it like a young Willie Mays and caught it — square between the eyes. The end result was two black eyes, a long conversation with the coach, and a move to second base where he played all four years... and another week off from typing class. Preacher often cited the football finger injury and baseball mishap as reasons why his typing skills as an adult were less than exemplary.

The baseball team at Barrickville was always good and Preacher's team won the conference title his sophomore through senior years. The mainstay was a pitcher named George White, a flame-thrower who also possessed a knee-buckling curve ball. Folks in the area always assumed White would sign a professional contract and someday pitch in the Major Leagues. Instead, as most of the young men in the community, he went to work in the mines the day after graduation.

One of the many highlights of Preacher's high school baseball career happened when he was a junior. Once again playing arch-rival Fairmont, Preacher came to bat late in the game with two runners on base and drove a ball over the center fielder's head. "Both runners scored and I drove in the winning run. I should have taken the next day off." Preacher didn't bother telling his parents about the hit when he got home that evening. He knew they wouldn't have been interested or even cared.

In his senior year, the coaches around the conference took notice of the excellent defensive second baseman from Barrickville. Both Preacher and White were named to the All-Conference team. Preacher was proud of the honor but, once again, it never came up in conversation with his parents.

Preacher considered his high school days to be somewhat ordinary. But that wasn't exactly the case. He passed all his classes (barely) and, in addition to playing three sports, also participated in the drama club. He thoroughly enjoyed being on stage and performing in front of an audience. And while neither of his parents ever saw him play a single game in high school, his mom did come to see him perform in one play.

Preacher never got the big parts, but that didn't keep him from sometimes stealing the show. He had trouble memorizing lines, and the teacher would spend extra time with him until he had everything down perfect. The plays would be held in the high school auditorium and practically everyone in town would come. In one play Preacher had a part where he would keep running in and out from behind the curtain yelling, "Where's my hat?" Although he couldn't remember the punch line, he did remember someone in the audience finally yelling back, "On your head, stupid!"

While it was true Preacher was living a life of sin, playing sports and being in the drama club would help him later in life. God saw something in this rough coal miner's son and was preparing him for the time when he would be speaking about the Lord Jesus Christ in front of audiences both small and large. Preacher just didn't know it yet.

As noted, Preacher was not the best student at Barrickville. But he did excel in mischief. Practical jokes were his specialty and most involved the principal whom he disliked. One morning in chemistry class Preacher and a few of his friends decided to mix iron filings and sulfuric acid in a fruit jar. They then sneaked down into the school's basement and put the concoction in the furnace. In a few minutes an odor that smelled like rotten eggs but only worse spread throughout the entire school. The principal never found out what made the awful odor and once again Preacher escaped punishment.

On another occasion, he and his friends put a heavy railroad tie in front of the principal's front door at home. Preacher recalled the man being barricaded inside for most of the day. Later, when the principal was out of town, Preacher, Ralph and Omer tied a cow on his front porch where she stayed for three days. When the principal returned, the porch was such a mess that he announced those responsible would be expelled from school. "He was so mad I thought he was going to kill everybody in school." In later years, Preacher often said if he had been caught doing half of the things he did while in high school, he would still be jail.

Halloween always presented Preacher and his friends with a chance to get into trouble. Preacher remembered a man named Montaque who owned an icehouse in town and was always yelling at the kids in the neighborhood. Every Oct. 31, Preacher would find some way to get even with him either by trick or treat... or simply by turning over all the man's outdoor toilets. One Halloween, Preacher and his gang covertly went to the home of the owner of the first Austin automobile in town, picked up the car and put it on the platform at the local barber shop. In making his escape, Preacher jumped on an old bicycle he had "acquired" and took off for home. A dog jumped out in front of him and over the handle bars Preacher went, landing squarely on his nose. "I must have plowed ten feet of ground. I chased that dog all over town but never caught him. I would have killed him on the spot if I could have only caught him." The next day Preacher had to go to school with his nose all scratched up. That wasn't so bad. Explaining how it got that way was a different matter.

High school was full of adventure for Preacher, but he knew there was still something missing in his life. "All through high school, I had no encounters with the Lord or religion at all. Mom and dad never went to church during the time I was in high school, and neither did my sister, Babe, or me." With no moral or spiritual compass at home, Preacher started developing bad habits. There was an old pool table at Peck's Garage and it is there Preacher would often go after school, practice or supper. "The pool sticks were about as crooked as a dog's hind leg. No problem, because the table was just about as crooked." A natural byproduct of shooting pool was betting on who would win. This was the beginning of an addiction Preacher would carry into his married life. By the time he graduated from high school, he was hooked. "I would bet on anything, whether a bird would land on this fence post or another." He also played cards. Whatever money he had he lost. Preacher also started drinking more, although the one habit he hadn't acquired yet was smoking. Coach Hamilton was dead set against it and any player caught was off the team.

Preacher never had a steady girlfriend in high school. The one girl he really liked dated the star of the basketball team, and he figured he had too many other things to worry about in his life anyway. He was getting ready to graduate, was doing double duty for the devil and had no real plans for his future. He was 17 years old and along with classmate Louis Hall, had been voted as the two seniors "least likely to succeed." Ironically, he and Louis would be the only ones in their class to ever graduate from college. The night of his high school graduation the only family member there was his mother. Preacher went home afterwards and cried. Again, he knew something was missing... he just couldn't figure out what.

Chapter 3

And Then I Met Freda

"And the peace of God, which transcends all understanding, will guard your hearts and your minds in Christ Jesus." **Mark 10:14 (NIV)**

There were lots of smiles, a few tears and plenty of hugs that night as the Barrickville High School class of 1933 took their first steps into the real world. Preacher experienced none of those as he accepted his diploma. He was 17 years old and had no idea what he was supposed to do next. Although his dad had mockingly mentioned college, Preacher knew he had enough schooling to last him a lifetime. And deep down, although he refused to admit it, he really did know where he would end up. So he did... nothing. Hanging around downtown Barrickville with no money and very little to do lasted about a month.

Sensing the inevitable, Preacher asked his dad to help him get a job in the coal mine. It wasn't long before he had his first job — a bit welder in the largest coal producing mine in West Virginia. For his efforts, he received 17 cents an hour and was often down in the mine for as many as 20 hours at a time. The work was hard, dirty and dangerous. A few weeks after he started, Preacher went down into the mine one day to do a small welding job. The only problem was he forgot to bring his torch lighter. He mentioned this to a co-worker and complained about having to go all the way back to the top of the mine to get it. The man, who had worked there for years, told Preacher there was an easier way. Preacher could catch a spark off the trolley line which carried 2,500 volts of electricity and light his torch that way. Soaking wet from sweat, Preacher put the torch on the electric arch and was promptly knocked flat on his back. "I tasted copper for two weeks. I probably should have been killed."

Preacher was a good worker and after a couple of months he got a generous pay raise of one cent and hour. The miners got paid every two weeks and often would get a receipt with nothing but "Xs" on it indicating they had already spent their entire paycheck in the company-owned store. By this time Preacher had become an opportunity drinker — "I drank whiskey every opportunity I got" — and often spent his money on alcohol and gambling.

Betting on pool, penny ante and on which way the wind would blow the next day, Preacher usually ran out of money before the next pay day. So he would go to the company store and get a book of script as an advance. Taking the script to a bootlegger, he would get 50 cents for each dollar of script. He would then play cards and lose that money or else drink it up. By now, Preacher had also acquired another habit to go along with gambling and drinking — smoking and chewing tobacco.

"I learned to smoke. I learned to chew. When I was inside, I chewed. When I was outside, I smoked."

The winter of 1933 was unusually cold even for mountains of West Virginia. And a pattern quickly emerged. Preacher would get up early in the morning and work all day. After showering at the mine and going home to dinner, he would go into Barrickville to shoot pool or play cards until bedtime. Most Saturdays he would spend the day drinking and horsing around with friends, becoming drunk by night fall. His drinking would continue throughout the weekend and he would always have trouble getting up on Monday mornings to go to work.

It was about this time that Preacher met Freda Johnston, who had just entered her sophomore year at Fairmont High School about eight miles from Barrickville. Preacher had gone to a high school basketball game and was talking to his old friend, Ralph, when Freda and another girl, Oneida Tarkington, walked up. Ralph was dating Oneida and introduced Preacher to Freda as "June Bug" Freeland. After talking for a few minutes, Preacher asked Freda if he could take her home after the game. She had come to Barrickville on the school bus and told Preacher as nicely as possible that she would be returning that very same way. Freda, who had just turned 15, would later tell Oneida that she didn't like Preacher. For his part, Preacher insisted it was he who turned down the chance to go out with Freda that night.

A few weeks later, Ralph asked Preacher if he wanted to drive to Fairmont in his old car and double date. Ralph was still seeing Oneida and Preacher's mystery date turned out to be Freda. The big evening out consisted of the four teenagers sitting on Oneida's front porch talking. At the end of the night Preacher walked Freda to the apartment where she was staying during the school year with her mother and sister. Although Freda's family lived on a farm near Crossroads, WV, her mother would take her two daughters and move into Fairmont during the school year so they could get a better education. After that first "date," Preacher and Freda decided they would continue seeing each other. Since he didn't own a car, Preacher would walk all the way to Fairmont with their dates usually consisting of sitting on the front porch of the apartment or going to a friend's house. Preacher noticed that Freda's mom usually set on a piano bench just inside the front window listening to their every conversation.

Preacher continued to date Freda during that school year and life started to take on new meaning for him. He was still working long hours in the coal mine. He was still drinking heavily. He was still smoking and chewing. And he was still gambling away his paychecks. But there was Freda. Several times each week, after working all day long, he would walk the eight miles to Fairmont and after visiting for an hour or so make the trek back home. Although Preacher was still serving the devil full-time, there seemed to be a peace when he was with Freda. And although he had never been to church or heard the Gospel of Jesus Christ, God was starting to put the pieces together for Preacher's life. Freda was not a Christian but her mother had always made sure she went to Sunday School. When Freda was about 12 years old, the pastor of a Methodist church asked if anyone wanted to come forward. She went to the front but nothing happened. No one prayed with her or even asked why she had come forward. She was baptized the next Sunday but in her heart, just like with Preacher, she knew something was missing.

After completing her sophomore year at Fairmont, Freda along with her mom and sister moved back to the family farm near Crossroads. Preacher had finally gotten himself a car by the time that summer came, and he would drive to see Freda two or three times a week. By now Freda realized Preacher was a special person, not knowing that he wrestled with demons just about every day. Because Preacher was a totally different man around her — a gentleman who treated her like a lady. Even Freda's parents liked Preacher and felt completely comfortable when he was around the house. In reflecting back, Freda often said Preacher really did a "snow job" on her mom and dad. During the entire time Preacher and Freda dated, she never had the opportunity to meet his parents and he rarely, if ever, spoke of them. Neither did she see the drinking, gambling and other vices that controlled Preacher's life.

Since Preacher had little money and what wasn't spent on alcohol, tobacco or gambling went towards putting gas in the car so he could visit Freda, their dates usually consisted of talking or visiting Freda's sister Ione and her husband Ralph. They lived about two miles from Freda's farm. One night when they were visiting Ralph jokingly asked, "Say, when are you two going to get married?" He then said, "I guess you're scared to get married." That was the first time the subject of marriage had come up, and not knowing what to say, both Preacher and Freda said in unison, "No we're not."

Later that evening, Preacher and Freda were sitting on Ralph and Ione's front porch talking about how much they enjoyed being with one another. Fall was coming in a couple of months and Freda's mother had decided to send her to Fairmont High alone that year. And Preacher's family had decided that he should go away to welding school so he would be able to get a better job in the mines. The thought of being away from each other was more than either of them could imagine, so they hatched a plan that would keep them together. They would get married. Knowing it would have to be before school started, they decided on a date in July. They also made another decision — they wouldn't tell either set of parents. Preacher was about to begin another chapter in his life, only this time, he would have someone to share it with.

Chapter 4

Who Said Marriage Was A Bed Of Roses?

"All the prophets testify about Him, that everyone who believes in Him receives forgiveness of sins through his name." **Acts 10:43 (NIV)**

Freda kept to the plan and did not tell her parents she intended to marry Preacher. But she did confide in her sister, Ione. On a hot summer Friday, Preacher picked up Freda and headed to Ralph and Ione's house. Freda had secretly taken her wedding dress there a few days earlier. And with that, all four piled into Preacher's old Ford and started the long drive to Oakland, MD. They arrived well after midnight and spent the early hours in a tourist home. Fifteen years old and under age, Freda lied about her age when they got their marriage license that Saturday morning in Oakland where no questions were asked.

With that out of the way, Preacher and Freda were directed to a Methodist minister, Rev. Davis, who married couples almost daily. Reverend Davis was sweeping his front porch and his wife was cleaning up after breakfast when they arrived at his home. Again, no questions were asked and Rev. Davis agreed to marry them as soon as he finished with his broom. Pastor Davis' wife, still in her apron, served as a witness to the marriage, while Ralph and Ione stood in as best man and woman. The ceremony only took a few minutes and, after a quick stop at a local restaurant, the four drove straight back to Fairmont. And that's how, on July 14, 1934, with an "invalid" marriage license, Preacher and Freda became Mr. & Mrs. Earl Freeland.

Once back in Fairmont, Preacher and Freda spent their honeymoon night in Ralph and Ione's home. The next day, they went to her parents' home where Freda's mother met her at the door crying. Her dad's reaction was more pragmatic, with his only words being, "You made the blister, now you sit on it." Not exactly the blessing Freda had hoped for but it would have to do. Surprisingly, Preacher was not privy to the brief conversation. Instead, he had decided to stay in the car with the windows rolled up. Better safe than sorry. As for Preacher's parents, they were separated by now and in the process of getting a divorce. So when he told his mother later that day what he had done, she said very little and instead went to bed saying she felt ill.

To say Preacher and Freda's marriage got off to a shaky start would be kin to saying Mount Vesuvius was nothing more than a small tremor. They moved in with Preacher's dad for the first few months, then settled on a one-bedroom rental in a home in Barrickville where they shared the kitchen with the owner. Freda knew absolutely nothing about cooking and had never washed or ironed a shirt. Preacher would leave early in the morning for the mines leaving Freda home alone all day. She would start cooking supper early in the afternoon, because more times than not, she would burn it and have to start over. About the only bright note was that Freda's parents had forgiven her somewhat and would come visit occasionally and bring food from the farm. Preacher and Freda rarely saw either one of his parents and when they did, they were usually drunk.

Preacher continued to drink heavily and gambled whenever he got the opportunity or had the money. Believing the husband was the head of the house and if you wanted to keep the marriage together you had to do what pleased him, Freda started doing the same things that Preacher did — drinking and smoking. But the more she sinned, the more God dealt with her. The only prayer Freda knew was "Now I lay me down to sleep" and she never went to bed, regardless of the hour, without reciting it first. Preacher thought that was hilarious.

A new chapter in Preacher and Freda's life opened up about 15 months later when their first child, Barbara, was born. The little baby girl was the apple of his eye, but not even she could break Preacher's sinful habits. He would take his paycheck to get food for the family and come back with nothing — all gambled away. In spite of the way he was living, Preacher still considered himself to be a good person. He saw no need to go to church and when Freda would occasionally suggest it, Preacher would change the subject. Instead, he would talk about the "good things" he did, like paying for movies for kids who couldn't afford it or helping people when they were down and out. And he would always bring up Mrs. Fleuhardy who lived just down the street and professed to be a good Christian. She religiously went to church but was better known as being the biggest gossiper in town — that's all Preacher saw. He once told Freda, "If Mrs. Fleuhardy is going to Heaven, then I don't want to. Besides, if I go to Hell, all of my friends will be there." The only answer Freda could think of was, "June, there are no friends in Hell."

When Barbara was still small, the Freelands moved into a house they shared with the owner, Mrs. Wilson. She was a real Christian and although she never talked to Preacher or Freda about the Lord, everything she did was Christ-like. Preacher would have friends over for a party and more often than not, things would get out of hand. Freda figured it was only a matter of time before Mrs. Wilson would ask them to leave. Instead, the next morning, she would knock on the door and be standing there with a freshly-baked loaf of bread or homemade pie and say, "I thought maybe you might like to have this." Every Sunday night they would see Mrs. Wilson pass by their window with her lantern walking to church. Freda saw the contrast in their lives but felt if she changed it would destroy her marriage and family. But things were only going to get worse.

Preacher was doing great at his job. He had a real knack for machinery and had been promoted from inside the mines to a topside shop where he ran a nine-inch precision lathe. At home it was a different story. The family moved 15 times in the next five years. If the landlord upset him, Preacher would get mad and immediately move out. They always lived in furnished apartments and never owned much more than the clothes on their backs.

In March 1940, Preacher and Freda's life became even more chaotic with the birth of their first son, Jim. I sincerely believe God has a timetable in mind for every one of us. For the Jews, it took 40 years for them to find their way out of the wilderness and into the Promised Land. The Freelands' timetable was marked not in years or days but instead in the number of apartments they had rented since eloping six years before. Because just after Jim was born, God led them to their "newest" basement apartment in Fairmont. It was time for the Freelands to stop messing around and find out exactly what that "something" was both had been missing. Only a couple of days after moving in, a neighbor named Mrs. Peebles showed up at the door completely unannounced and invited Freda to go to church with her later that night. She explained that an evangelist, who had been a Broadway dancer with the musical revue *"George White Scandals,"* was going to give her personal testimony about how she came to know the Lord. Freda couldn't believe that someone who had worked in New York City and even on Broadway would drop all of that and become an evangelist. So, after talking Preacher into watching Barbara and Jim that evening, Freda told Mrs. Peebles "yes."

After thanking Mrs. Peebles and closing the door, Freda's mind immediately began racing. And naturally her first thought was, "What am I going to wear? This isn't a night club." Going through her closet, she found some orange shoes and a black dress with long sleeves — just what she believed a Christian would wear. She already knew how to act having been in a church before, so she figured the people there would never know she wasn't like them.

That night Freda and Mrs. Peebles walked to the Christian & Missionary Alliance Church on Water Street in Fairmont. After the service started, an elderly man prayed, "Lord, bless the stranger in our gates tonight." Freda knew immediately she was that stranger. After the singing, the evangelist gave her testimony. Invited to try out for a new musical revue in downtown New York City, she had been given the wrong address and when she got out of the taxi, found she was in front of an Alliance church. By that point it was too late to get to the audition. Thinking she might as well go back home, she got ready to get back in the taxi when she heard singing coming from the church. It was the most beautiful Gospel song she'd ever heard so she decided to go in. Before she left that night, she had accepted Jesus Christ as her personal Savior and immediately gave up her career to study for the ministry.

After finishing her testimony, the evangelist invited those who wanted prayer to raise their hands. Thinking, "I'm not going to raise my hand," Freda heard the woman say, "Yes, thank you." Freda had raised her hand without even realizing it.

By the time the evangelist had invited those who wanted to meet the Lord to come forward, Freda was already halfway down the isle. Unlike when she was 12 years old, someone knelt down beside her and led her to a saving knowledge of the Lord Jesus Christ. Afterwards when the evangelist invited Freda to tell the congregation what the Lord had done for her, she responded, "The Lord forgave me of my sins and now I'm a child of God."

Walking back home from the meeting with Mrs. Peebles, Freda saw a friend she had known in high school across the street. Excited about her new life in Christ, she yelled over and asked the girl how she was doing. When the girl responded that she was doing fine and asked Freda how she was doing, she cried, "Great! I just got saved!"

Chapter 5

Who Needs Religion? I Do!

"And my God will meet all your needs according to His glorious riches in Christ Jesus." **Philippians 4:19 (NIV)**

When Freda walked into the house that early summer night in 1940, Preacher was rocking Jim to sleep while Barbara was playing with her few toys on the floor. The first thing Freda did was take the cigarettes out of her pocket and lay them on the mantel. With tears in her eyes, she told Preacher, "I won't be needing these any more. I was saved tonight." Although she was a brand new Christian, Freda knew she would never again take a sip of alcohol or spend half the night dancing in some smoke-filled night club. And she knew Barbara would never have to climb into her lap again and beg her not to light up a cigarette. The sins that had become such a regular part of her life were gone. She had been delivered from them the second she kneeled down to pray and had even told the Lord, "If I ever put another cigarette in my mouth, I hope you will strike me dead."

Preacher, of course, had a lot less "faith" in her and thought it was all a big joke, telling her, "Oh yeah, you got religion. That will last a couple of weeks and then everything will be back to normal." But it did last. After the revival, Freda continued to go to the Alliance church every Sunday and would take Barbara and Jim with her. Preacher, meantime, would spend his Sunday mornings at the pool hall. Every night Freda would go into the bathroom to pray. It was located right next to the kitchen and Preacher would rattle dishes, drop pans on the floor and make as much noise as he could. "It's a wonder the Lord didn't strike me dead. I'm so ashamed for the way I acted, but I resented what was happening and would do anything for it to be the way it used to be."

Preacher did his very best over the next few months to make Freda's life as miserable as possible. He continued drinking with his buddies and would even bring alcohol into the house. He would light up a cigarette and blow the smoke in Freda's face to try to entice her to start up again. And he continued to make as much noise as he could when she would pray in the bathroom. In his mind, if he made enough racket, maybe her prayers wouldn't be heard in Heaven.

But what Preacher didn't know was that the people in the Fairmont Alliance Church were praying for him, as well. And although he was still sinning as hard as he could, God was dealing with his heart. Preacher was miserable and he didn't even know why. "I was so miserable. I'll never forget. I can close my eyes and walk to the very point and see myself standing there. My face was black with coal dust and tears coursing down my cheeks. I didn't know why except that I knew I was miserable and that I didn't have what my wife had."

The old saying " the calm before the storm" certainly applied to Preacher by this point — but only if you change the phrase completely around. The more Freda and the folks at the Alliance church prayed, the more he lashed out. "I had a temper like a wild cat." Any mention at all by Freda about church would set him off. He remembered one Sunday, after Freda had asked him if he would like to join her and the kids, pounding on the kitchen table so hard that the cups and saucers bounced up and down on it. In a rage, he told Freda to go to church any time she wanted, but never to ask him to go again. She never did.

It seemed like everything Freda did made him angry. One afternoon Preacher was sitting on the couch plunking away on an old mandolin when Freda brushed by and gave him a love tap on the back of the head with a magazine. He was so wound up and defensive of her every move that he took the neck of the mandolin and beat it up and down on the floor until there was nothing left but the strings in his hand. He then went to a jewelry store and bought himself another one. "Talk about dumb. Talk about ignorant. Buddy, that was me all over and over again."

But God was just getting started with June Bug. Later that year, Preacher was talking to a friend of his in the mine who he had played basketball with in high school. This friend was now playing in a local league for the Methodist church in town. He invited Preacher to join the team but there was one catch: Preacher would have to come to Sunday School. It was a church rule. Preacher missed playing basketball, so he agreed and ended up attending Sunday School there for the next several months, often taking Barbara with him. In all the weeks he visited there, never once did Preacher hear the name of Jesus Christ used and never once did the Sunday School teacher tell him that He was a wonderful Savior and available to him. But, as Preacher recalled, he did get to talk about sports for a good hour in that class every Sunday.

Freda continued to pray for Preacher, asking the Lord to convict him of his sins. One Sunday night Preacher asked Freda to go roller-skating but she declined and he went alone. She remembered praying that the Lord would make him miserable. "Wouldn't you know, he won the door prize that night and it was a pair of roller skates. He came home with them over his shoulder so proud." On other occasions Preacher would take Barbara to the movies or go out alone to shoot pool. And as soon as he would leave, Freda would get on her knees and pray until she thought it was time for him to come back.

By now Preacher's parents were divorced and his mother, now a full-blown alcoholic, would often stay with him and Freda. Like Preacher, she made fun of Freda's religion and one day as she was leaving, told her, "You'd better stop this or you're going to lose your family." Freda replied, "Mahalia, Christ has done something for me and He's the most important thing in my life, and if it costs me everything

I have, even my home, my life belongs to God."

Not long after that, the tension caused by Freda's acceptance of the Lord came to a tipping point. Preacher had done everything he could to make her return to the life she once led. But the Lord had changed her life completely and nothing Preacher could say or do would change that. Finally, after giving Freda a particularly hard time one night, she turned to Preacher and said, "Honey, I love you and I love the Lord, and I want you to know if I have to give you up, I will, but I'm going to serve Him." It was like he had been bulldozed by that same mule of a fullback in high school all over again. Freda, Barbara and Jim meant everything in the world to Preacher and the thought of losing them kept him awake at nights for the rest of the week. When Saturday came and everybody in the family was sitting around the dinner table, Preacher dropped a bombshell: he told Freda that he and Barbara would being going to church with her the next morning.

The devil knows he can't win but he certainly does like trying. The next morning, Jim woke up sick and Freda was unable to go to Sunday School or church. In spite of this, Preacher kept his word and him and Barbara went to the Alliance church. In an adult Sunday School class that morning, Preacher heard about the love of Jesus for the very first time. It shook him to the core. He left before it was over and hurried to Barbara's Sunday School class, telling her teacher he wasn't feeling well and was going to take her home. When he got home, he told Freda just the opposite — that Barbara had gotten sick in Sunday School so he had to bring her home early. In truth, Preacher would have said or done anything to get out of that Sunday School class. He had heard something that unnerved him and couldn't possibly be true. His heavenly Father loved him.

Jim was feeling better by that afternoon and as Freda prepared for the Sunday evening service, she noticed Preacher getting ready, too. Thinking he was probably headed to the pool hall or some place else, she asked where he was going. He simply replied, "With you." But Preacher wasn't going down quite that easily. After getting dressed, he gathered every cigar, cigarette, pipe and tobacco pouch he could find and stuffed them in his front pockets where everyone would see them. Arriving at church, he defiantly strolled up the middle isle and plopped himself down two rows from the front. If God was looking to pick a fight, he was ready. "Thinking back, when we went into church that night, I was too dumb to sit in the back where I could sneak out." Although Preacher may have sensed something was up, he had no idea he was about to find what he'd been looking for his entire life.

Chapter 6

A New Creature In Christ

"Here I stand at the door and knock. If anyone hears my voice and opens the door, I will come in and eat with him, and he with me." **Revelations 3:20 (NIV)**

After Preacher and his family had been seated, Rev. Mark Baines, pastor of the Fairmont Christian & Missionary Alliance Church, opened the service with prayer. And then the singing began. "Well, I listened to them sing that night. Man, I tell you, I never heard singing like that in all my life. I was so taken with the way they were singing those Gospel songs, I turned around to see if the people were really meaning what they were singing." Preacher knew in his heart, or at least in his gut, the congregation believed every word. One song in particular, written in 1899 by Lewis E. Jones, tore at his soul — *"There is Power in the Blood."*

> *Would you be free from the burden of sin?*
> *There's pow'r in the blood, pow'r in the blood;*
> *Would you o'er evil a victory win?*
> *There's wonderful pow'r in the blood.*

After the song service, several people in the congregation stood up and told what the Lord meant to them. It was the first time Preacher had ever heard a testimony, and he wasn't quite sure what to make of it. He looked around each time someone stood up, often recognizing people he knew either from the community or from the mine. He listened carefully to each word, secretly hoping he would catch someone telling a lie. The more he listened, the more uncomfortable he got. But again, deep inside, he knew every man, woman and child who had stood up spoke nothing but the truth. When the testimonies ended, Preacher quickly scanned the sanctuary for a quick avenue of escape. But since he had been so sure of himself, getting up and walking all the way back up that center aisle wasn't an option. So he sat there as Rev. Baines began his sermon.

Although he didn't, Rev. Baines could have easily entitled his sermon that night, "This is the Life of Earl Freeland." The message was so personal and direct that Preacher found himself glancing repeatedly at Freda to see if she looked guilty. He thought for sure she had told Rev. Baines all about him because he was quoting his life. "All he was doing was talking about a sinner, and that's what I was."

It began with a tug. Then a pull. And by the midway point of the sermon, Preacher felt as if a vice had been clamped down on his heart. God was tired of messing around with Earl Walter Freeland. Preacher began thinking of all the sin in his life and how much pain it was causing Freda and the children. He had come in arrogant and prideful. Now the only thing he felt was ashamed. Before Preacher knew what was happening, the congregation began singing an invitation hymn... one that had been written many years before by Charlotte Elliott and seemingly just for him:

> *Just as I am, without one plea,*
> *But that Thy blood was shed for me,*
> *And that Thou bid'st me come to Thee,*
> *O Lamb of God, I come! I come!*

Emotions welled up in Preacher when Rev. Baines gave the invitation. He asked those who needed prayer to raise their hand so the church body could pray for them. When Rev. Baines acknowledged that a request had been made, Preacher looked up and saw it was his own hand lifted high in the air. He pulled it down as quickly as he could, but by that time, it was too late. People in the church started praying — praying for Preacher. There was an awesome sense of the presence of God in the church that night. Filled nearly to capacity at the beginning of the service, not one person had left the building.

When Pastor Baines gave an open invitation for anyone needing to come to the alter and seek the Lord, Preacher was on his feet. "It was like the Holy Spirit lifted me out of my seat and I found myself walking down the isle." When he got to the altar, "I hit it like a wet sack of oats. I tell you, if anyone came near to drowning in their own tears, it was me that night." Reverend Baines knelt on one side of Preacher and a white-headed elder, Bob Dennis, knelt on the other. After they prayed, Pastor Baines shared the plan of salvation from the scriptures with Preacher and led him to the Lord. Although Preacher knew very little about being saved, he recognized immediately that God had met his heart's need. When asked to tell the congregation what had happened, Preacher turned to the audience and through tear-stained eyes and cheeks said, "I don't know what's happened to me tonight, but I know something wonderful has." Preacher had become a new creature in Christ.

Chapter 7

Through With Those Awful Habits

"Do your best to present yourself to God as one approved, a workman who does not need to be ashamed and who correctly handles the world of truth." **Timothy 2:15 (NIV)**

Preacher's feet never touched the ground that night as he walked home from church with his family. The weight of the world — and a lifetime of sins — had been lifted off him and he felt like he was floating on air. Him and Freda discussed what had happened as they got ready for bed. Knowing how the Lord had delivered her from smoking and drinking, Freda said, "You won't be going to the pool hall, and gambling, and doing of those other things, will you?" Rubbing his chin, Preacher responded, "Yeah, why yeah. I won't be gambling anymore but I might just go down the pool hall once in a while." As if scolding one of their children, she looked him square in the eye and said, "Oh no you won't." And then a wonderful thing happened. Preacher had never prayed about anything in his life, but at that moment he turned to her and said, "Let's pray about it."

The Holy Spirit was already teaching him what in meant to trust in the Lord. When you have a problem, when you need answers, when you need assurances, when you need wisdom, when you just need a friend to talk to... you pray. So they got down on their knees together beside the bed. Not knowing exactly what to do or say, Preacher prayed to himself and asked God to show His will for his life. When he had finished his simple prayer, he got up and knew he was through with his life of sin. "Honey, you're right. I'm through with all those awful things I've been doing." And just like Freda had done several months before, he emptied the cigarettes, cigars, pipe and tobacco out of his pockets and put them on the table. Remembering that night years later, Preacher said, "As far as I'm concerned, all those things are still sitting on that table today."

The world had changed overnight when he woke the next morning. Preacher was convinced the grass was greener and that the birds sang prettier. He didn't even care which fence pole the birds landed on. Somebody gave Preacher a Gideon's pocket New Testament Bible and he started taking it to work. There was a large lumber pile in the back of the mine where some of the guys would each their lunch — the same guys Preacher had been drinking whiskey, shooting pool and gambling with just a few weeks before. It didn't take them long before they noticed something had changed about Preacher. Each day, he would take the little Bible out of his pocket and read it to himself. It didn't take long for some of his co-workers to start asking him questions about the "book." Not knowing what to do, he simply would read verses to them. And though Preacher had never witnessed to anyone before, he wasn't ashamed to tell them about his Savior. The guys would cuss and Preacher would talk about the Lord — it made for some great discussions. It wasn't many months before Preacher had practically worn that New Testament out.

Meanwhile, Preacher, Freda and the kids were going to the Alliance church every Sunday. It was a about a mile walk there and Preacher remembered making that trek holding Barbara and Jim's hands in all kinds of bad weather. It seemed like it rained or snowed every Sunday but that just made him more determined to get there and learn more about the Lord. Whenever Preacher had a question about the scriptures, Pastor Baines would patiently sit down with him and explain God's message. And then they would pray. Preacher settled many truths early on that he would carry into his ministry with the loving help of Rev. Baines.

A few months after Preacher was saved, the Sunday School director at Alliance asked him to teach a class of six junior high boys. "Brother, I'm telling you, they were more 'wild cat' than boy." Preacher found out several months later that no one else in the church would teach the class and that's why he had been asked. God gave Preacher a special kind of love for those young boys and he would spend hours studying so he could teach them about Jesus. In no time, the class grew from a half dozen to 16 boys. Then came news that the Sunday School was going to hold a contest to see which class could increase their attendance the most in three months' time. The teacher of the winning class would receive a real study Bible, and since Preacher needed one, he urged his boys to start bringing their friends. At the end of the contest, there were 36 of the most mischievous, rambunctious, and in Preacher's eyes, most precious little fellas in the world crammed into his classroom. Preacher now had the biggest Bible in the whole county.

About a year later Preacher became the youth leader at Fairmont Alliance Church. And he kept his Sunday School class. And though he felt no special call on his life other than a desire to serve the Lord in the church, God was preparing Preacher for an even bigger purpose.

Chapter 8

Growing In Grace

"Let us not give up meeting together, as some are in the habit of doing, but let us encourage one another, and all the more as you see the day approaching."
Hebrews 10:25 (NIV)

Preacher was quite content to continue teaching his Sunday School class and leading the youth of the church. He felt like he was in the will of God and his horizon stretched no farther than Fairmont, WV. He figured he would continue to work in the mine, raise his family and be active in his home church. God had delivered he and Freda from a life of sin and he would serve the Lord right there in that small town the rest of his life. Obviously God did not get Preacher's memo.

By mid-1942 Preacher and Freda were filled with mixed emotions. On one hand, things were going great with his job at the mine. They were both active in serving the Lord and Freda was expecting their third child in December. But Preacher also was heavily burdened. Preacher's parents were now divorced and Mahalia had been diagnosed with cancer. His mom's condition continued to worsen and late in the year she was hospitalized. Preacher visited her as often as possible.

One late afternoon and still in his dusty work clothes, Preacher stopped by the hospital. Mahalia was going to need blood, and as they talked, Preacher mentioned he was going to donate a pint or so before he left. His mother begged him not to, thinking it might somehow be dangerous to his health. At that very instant, Preacher was pressed by the Holy Spirit to witness to his mother one more time. An alcoholic who had never attended a church service as best as Preacher could remember, she had rejected his efforts to tell her about Jesus and his love dozens of times before. Preacher told his mother that the small amount of blood he could give was nothing compared to the blood that Jesus shed for her on Calvary. And then, filthy from a day at the mine, he led her to a saving knowledge of the Lord Jesus Christ. Mahalia died a few weeks later and went to be with the Lord.

Preacher and Freda's third child, Earl, was born Dec. 29, 1942. Between work, spending time with the family and working with the youth at the church, Preacher had very few free hours to spare. But as busy as he was, he always found time to go fishing or play softball with the men from the church. However, whenever Preacher would ask Pastor Baines to join them, he never seemed to have enough time. There was always too much to be done around the church. And though his ministry prospered, the strain of all work and no play finally got to him and he had to leave the church for health reasons. Without realizing it at the time, Preacher learned a lesson he would carry throughout his entire ministry — there has to be time for relaxation.

Fairmont Alliance was without a pastor for about six months. During that period, elders or other church leaders filled in the best they could on Sunday mornings and evenings. Even Preacher took his turn a couple of times delivering the morning message. Finally, Rev. D.W. Klaus, an older minister from Michigan, accepted the position. The people in the church, and especially Preacher and Freda, learned to love him. A real people's person, Rev. Klaus made it a point to get to know his congregation on a personal basis.

One Saturday afternoon, Preacher and fellow church member, Jennings Manley, took Rev. Klaus fishing. Preacher may have given up his sinful ways when he was saved, but he still liked a good practical joke. After Rev. Klaus threw his line in, Preacher secretly cast his in and hooked Rev. Klaus' with his own. He then gave it a great big tug. Reverend Klaus jumped up and yelled, "Boys, I got me a big one." After playing with the line a few minutes, Preacher gave a another big pull and broke Rev. Klaus' line. "I just lost the biggest fish of my life" he moaned over and over. Preacher and Manley never told him what had really happened.

A Christian now for almost three years, the Lord began to work in Preacher's life in a special way. He wanted to spend more time in prayer so he approached Manley about starting a prayer meeting after work. Manley, who had accepted Christ about the same time Preacher had, was a crane operator in the mill next to the mine, and he and Preacher got off work about the same time each afternoon. They agreed they would meet after work at the Alliance church, just the two of them. The two brothers in Christ had some great times with the Lord, praising Him and asking God to meet the needs of the church. After praying, and with lunch buckets under their arms, they would go home. "Sometimes I was as dirty as two hogs ought to have been." It was during one of these prayer sessions that God asked Preacher a very important question. Thinking he must have too much coal dust in his ears and hadn't heard correctly, he got up and left.

Chapter 9

Called? Who Me?

"Are not two sparrows sold for a penny, yet not one of them falls to the ground apart from the will of your Father. And even the very hairs on your head are numbered. So don't be afraid. You are worth more than many sparrows." **Matthew 10:29-31 (NIV)**

Our timing and God's timing aren't always on the same clock. After praying with Manley, Preacher started home when he heard a voice saying, "Son, will you go into full-time work for me?" The voice was so clear and plain that Preacher stopped dead in his tracks. It wasn't everyday somebody stopped him on the street to offer him a job. When Preacher turned around, there was no one there. So he started walking again. He hadn't gone but a few steps when he heard the voice again, "Son, will you go into full-time service for me?" Preacher had never considered himself to be the sharpest tool in the shed but this time he recognized that voice. "Lord, you can't mean someone like me! You just can't mean me." He stood there on the sidewalk with tears running down his cheeks. With a limited education, a wife and now three children, the thought of going into the ministry just wasn't possible. Besides, World War II was going on and Preacher was in what the U.S. Army called a defense critical job. His deferment from active service was dependent on him staying employed in the coal mine. Pondering these things, Preacher walked the rest of the way home with tears still pouring down his face. "If someone had seen me they would have thought I was drunk or stupid or something." When he got home, Preacher didn't say a word to Freda about what had happened. But he did tell the Lord, "If you will make it as plain to my wife without me telling her, I'll do it."

Preacher continued to read his Bible during lunch hour and meet with Manley after work for prayer. God honored his faithfulness and he was able to lead two of his co-workers to the Lord. One afternoon while running his lathe, Preacher started thinking about God's call on his life and doubts started creeping in. He started listing all the reasons he could think of why going into the ministry full-time would never be possible, and he even remembered what his dad had told him a few short weeks before: "Hey, the insane asylum at Western is full of crazy people. Don't go too far with this religion thing."

Frustrated, confused and a little angry at both himself and God, Preacher picked up the New Testament he kept lying beside the lathe and turned to the Gospel of Matthew. He read where Jesus talked about the will of the Father and how He knew even when a sparrow fell to the ground. After reading the verse, "So don't be afraid. You are worth more than many sparrows," Preacher was immediately drawn to a commotion outside the little window in the lathe room. When he looked out, a whole flock of sparrows was flying by. There must have been a million of them. Fighting back tears, Preacher thanked the Lord that he was valued more than many sparrows and for being there when he needed Him most.

Nearly a month went by and Preacher still had not mentioned his call to the ministry to anyone. One Sunday evening before church, Preacher and some other men were talking outside when Joe Perry, who operated the Union Rescue Mission across the street, walked up. Preacher had helped Perry on several occasions and they had become close friends. With all the fellas standing around, Perry turned and looked Preacher right in the eye. "I'll never forget that little buzzard. He said to me, 'Freeland, has God called you to Preach?' Well, I could feel the red going to my ears, you know. I didn't want to be embarrassed by these guys and I said, 'Oh, I don't know. Something like that.'" But Perry wasn't finished. He then said, "I'll tell you what. Until he does, I've got a little church out here in the country. I want you to come out and preach for a week." Preacher told him he had lost his marbles and must be out of his mind, plus a few other choice reasons why it was impossible. Perry replied, "It doesn't make any difference. God told me to ask you." Preacher agreed to preach two of the five services.

The night of the first service, Preacher got into his old car and, after tying the doors together to keep them from flying open when he went around a corner, spit and sputtered his way down a dirt road to the little country church. Driving and talking to the Lord at the same time, Preacher decided to put out another fleece. He told the Lord he still wasn't sure he had been called to the ministry and Freda had not said anything about it. He then told the Lord that if someone accepted Him as their personal Savior that night, he would believe he had truly been called. Preacher was pretty pleased with himself after that. He figured someone getting saved from a message he preached was about the most improbable thing he could ask of God. For the first time in his life, Preacher knew he had placed a bet he simply couldn't lose.

Preacher recalled never being so nervous in his life. In fact, he couldn't remember then or even years later what he said that night from the pulpit. But he somehow got through his sermon and gave the altar call. Six people were at the altar before the first verse of the invitational hymn was finished. And each and every one of them came to know the Lord Jesus Christ as their Savior. As he started back down the dirt road headed for home, Preacher pulled over and thanked God. "Lord, I'm convinced that you have called me into the ministry. All you have to do now is convince my wife." Preacher was still hedging his bets.

A few weeks later, while sitting in a Sunday night service at Alliance, the Lord began dealing with him again. Slipping out of his seat, Preacher went to the altar and began to pray. A short while later Freda knelt beside him and Preacher heard her prayer: "Okay Lord, even if it means being a preacher's wife." That sealed it for him. The two got up from the altar and hugged each other right there in the middle of the church. After the service, they stayed behind and talked to Rev. Klaus about Preacher's call to the ministry.

Reverend Klaus was encouraging... but also blunt. He had graduated from the Alliance denomination's Nyack Missionary Training Institute in Nyack, NY, years before and told Preacher going to college to study for the ministry wouldn't be easy. First, he said, you will have to trust God for all your needs. And second, don't expect any financial help from the people back home. Knowing it was God's will, Preacher applied to Nyack and a few weeks later received a letter telling him he had been accepted to the freshman class that would be starting in September 1944. But the news wasn't all good. The letter also stated that there were no apartments available. If Preacher wanted to enroll, he would have to come alone and live in the dorm.

The euphoria of being accepted to Nyack lasted about a nanosecond before reality delivered a nasty sucker punch right in Preacher's gut. He and Freda had been living hand-to-mouth their entire married life and didn't have a red cent in the bank. Freda had never worked a day in her life and Preacher would obviously have to give up his job in the mine. Still, he was determined to do the will of the Lord and Freda supported him fully.

There was also the matter of the draft board. Preacher remembered marching into the draft board office a week or so later and informing the lady in charge that he had been saved by the Lord and was going to college in Nyack, NY. "She just reared back and said, 'You're in a critical industry, and that's what your deferment is for. You leave the coal mine and I'll have you in the Army next week.'" Preacher calmly replied, "Well, that's how it will have to be." And then he started witnessing to her. He told her how the Lord and changed his life, met his needs and called him to the ministry that afternoon on the sidewalk. Then he said, "Mam, I have to obey the call of God on my life. If it works out that you put me in the Army, I'll consider that God's will and I'll go to school after I've served my time, but I've got to obey God." By the time Preacher had finished, you would have thought the Hoover Dam had busted. Sobbing almost uncontrollably, she told Preacher she was the chairman of the draft board and not to worry. His deferment would be transferred so that he could go to college.

But that still didn't solve the money issue. How would he afford the tuition? Or feed his family or pay the rent? So Preacher and Freda got down on their knees beside the bed for the millionth time and started to pray. God laid it on both their hearts that He would provide for their needs. With that settled, they decided Preacher would go to school, get a job and totally support himself. Freda, in return, would get a job and keep the family afloat back home. Great plan. The only problem being Freda had never worked a day in her life and didn't even have a high school education.

Westinghouse, a manufacturing company founded in the late 1800s and still prominent today under the Westinghouse Electric Company name, had a plant just outside Fairfield. Freda learned they were hiring and, after taking a test, stood outside the plant with about 100 other people who had applied for 20 jobs. She was chosen. That night, she thanked the Lord but also reminded Him she had no one to look after her children while she worked. The next Sunday, a lady and her daughter at church came up to her and asked, "You need someone to watch the kids? We will do it." Freda had not said a word to anybody about needing a baby-sitter. Freda then explained she had no car and no way to pick them up or take them home. The lady said not to worry. They would get there somehow and if for some reason Freda needed to work overtime, they would just stay through the night. Another prayer answered.

Freda went to work at Westinghouse three days before Preacher left for Nyack connecting and welding parts on an assembly line. Her first day on the job was hectic. After walking a mile to the bus to get to work, she stood on her feet all day long. When she got home that evening she fell into a big lounge chair thinking she would never be able to do this every day. When Preacher got home, he found her still sitting there crying. It nearly broke his heart.

Two days later, Rev. Klaus took Preacher, Freda and the three children to the train station. Preacher had never been away from his wife and children, and he had never traveled to a big city. After an emotional good-bye, Preacher waited for his train on the platform, sitting on his one small suitcase while weeping like a baby. Other than the old black suit he was wearing, the only other clothing he carried was one pair of work pants and one work shirt. "There was never a 'greener' guy who walked off a train as I was that day in New York City."

Chapter 10

Aren't You Kind Of Old?

"As Jesus was walking beside the sea of Galilee, he saw two brothers, Simon, called Peter, and his brother Andrew. They were casting a net into the lake, for they were fishermen. 'Come, follow me,' Jesus said, 'and I will make you fishers of men.' At once they left their nets, and followed him." **Matthew 4:18-20 (NIV)**

Parents who've had kids go off to college for the first time know move-in day is, at best, disorganized chaos. I've often believed colleges make it that way so parents will forget how sad they are about junior or sissy leaving home and concentrate more on getting out of there as fast as possible. With only one small suitcase and no entourage to say goodbye to, Preacher didn't have to worry about anything like that. But as he got off the bus at Nyack Missionary Training Institute, Preacher did experience one thing just about every first-year student does when he or she arrives on campus — panic. "There I was, blind as a bat and dumb as a zebra." At the registrar's office, he enrolled as a full-time student to study becoming a preacher and pastor. A 28-year-old coal miner with a wife and three children back home and not a penny to his name, Preacher didn't exactly fit the profile of a normal student. After finishing up the paperwork, he was given a tiny room in the men's dormitory. It took him about a second to unpack and then he spent the rest of the afternoon helping other students carry their suitcases and trunks into the dorm. "They were so heavy they must have had everything but the kitchen sink in them."

Later, As he sat down for the evening meal in the school cafeteria, Preacher finally had time to reflect back on the past few days. Thinking about how much he already missed his wife and children back in Fairmont was almost too much for him. And then he remembered scripture in Matthew in which Jesus had called two fishermen, Simon Peter and Andrew, and said to them, *"Come follow me and I will make you fishers of men."* Come follow me, he said to himself, the same exact call he had received and one he was just beginning to fulfill.

After dinner, the students returned to their dorm rooms to spend a last night of freedom from study before classes began the next day. All except Preacher. The school had agreed to hire him for 20 cents an hour so he could pay his tuition. As he would do every night that first year, Preacher went down into the basement and fired up the coal furnaces so the dormitory and students would stay warm. He kept himself busy for the next few hours by cleaning the boiler room and carrying out ashes, all the while thinking about Freda and his children. Meanwhile, back in Fairmont, Freda had just put the children to bed and was on her knees by the bed. She asked God to watch over Barbara, Jim and Earl, and to take especially good care of Preacher. For the first night since their marriage, she and Preacher were apart. Her heart nearly broke.

Preacher got his course schedule the next morning... and gulped. He read down the long list of topics he would have to cover that first year: English, Homiletics (he didn't even know what that word meant), History of Missions, Historical Geography, Old Testament Survey, Literature, Parliamentary Procedure, Life of Christ, Music Fundamentals and Physical Education. That night, Preacher again went to the furnace room and began his chores. He also did something he'd rarely done in high school. He studied. "I had been out of school for years and my best subject back then had been recess and pulling pranks. I got an A+ in mischief."

Freda had also settled down into a routine after a few days of Preacher being gone. She would get up at five o'clock every morning, get Barbara ready for school, and then leave for work. She didn't have an alarm clark and trusted the Lord to awaken her. "I'd wake up every morning at the exact same time and was never late for work. And another strange thing happened. Every day a wren would come and peck on my window. It was as though God was saying, 'Don't worry. I'll take care of you.'" After work and the bus ride and walk home, Freda would take care of the kids and spend time playing with them until it was their bedtime. She would then pick up the letter from Preacher — there was one on her plate just about every afternoon when she arrived home from work — and read about how his classes were going or how he had gotten a job cutting someone's lawn for extra money. And as always, she would read how much he loved her and the children. Although there wasn't much to say, Freda never missed a day writing Preacher, either, telling him how the children were doing and how much everybody loved him. Since there was no telephone at home, Freda did not talk to Preacher but one time that first semester.

She remained active in the church and never missed a service, wearing out the one mile route on foot. When they crossed the street, Jim would take hold of her skirt on one side and Earl would grab the other. Barbara was old enough by now to look out for herself. Freda kept the people in the church up-to-date on how Preacher was doing in school. And then finally it was the holiday season — time for Christmas and Preacher to come home.

As the train carrying Preacher back to Fairmont rumbled along, he reflected on the four months since he had left home for college. Every day had been hectic. Going to school during the day, doing odd jobs in the late afternoon, and firing up the furnaces and studying late into the night had taken a toll on him. He was getting only a few hours of sleep and often missed meals because he was working. Still, Preacher was satisfied with what he had accomplished. His test scores were good and he found the many hours he had spent preparing to teach the Sunday School class of young boys back in Fairmont had helped him develop disciplined study habits. And he was more convinced than ever that he was in God's will. "I never questioned the call of God on my life. God had to take special care of me because he knew how stupid I was." After what seemed like a lifetime, the train finally pulled into the station. If he hadn't been so tired, he would have leaped for joy.

Freda had dressed the children in their Sunday-best clothes. The house was spotless and she couldn't wait for him to walk through the front door. But the promise of a glorious homecoming didn't exactly go off as planned. When Preacher walked in, little Earl started crying and grabbed Freda by the leg, yelling, "Mommy, there's a strange man in the house." It was more than Preacher and Freda could take and both broke down and cried. "We both just fell apart," Freda remembered. "He felt bad and I felt bad. We both looked like skin and bones. He looked so weak and I did, too. He stayed through that Christmas and I don't think either of us knew what we were going to do the next half year." One thing was certain, though. If Preacher was to return to Nyack, he would have to walk there. They didn't have a penny to their name for his train fare back.

A few days after Christmas, Preacher received a message from one of the men at the mine asking him to stop by and visit. Preacher went the next day and enjoyed a couple of hours talking with the guys and laughing about old times. They teased him about being a "Preacher Boy" and told him some people would do anything to keep from working. Preacher knew they were just messing with him and loved every second of it. As he was leaving the shop to go back home, the fellas handed Preacher an envelope. Inside was enough money for his train ride back to Nyack and his tuition for the next semester. God had answered another prayer. As poor as church mice, Preacher and Freda knelt down beside their bed once again and thanked the Lord for His bountiful blessings.

Preacher enjoyed the rest of his Christmas break and was even able to get a part-time job for a few weeks driving a truck for the Union Missions. He was grateful for the opportunity to make a few extra dollars, but it came at a price. There was no window in the truck door and the cold air caused Preacher to get Bell's palsy, a disorder of the nerve that controls movement of the muscles in the face. It would be the only physical problem Preacher would have during his three years of college.

Returning to Nyack for his second semester, Preacher once again settled into his familiar routine. The money he had been given from his friends at the mine along with his job at school allowed him to pay off all his debts to the college for the first year. And although there was no money for he and Freda to talk by telephone, they continued to write each other every day. Juggling classes, work and studying was a real struggle, but he continued to make good grades and even found time occasionally to spend with his younger classmates. The only topics that gave Preacher real trouble were English and especially Literature. He and some of the other students in the class made a pact that the day the Literature class ended for the year, they would all go down to the river and throw their books in. Preacher blamed a little of the "June Bug" mischief coming out for that one.

By the end of his first year at Nyack, Preacher's one black suit looked like a hand-me-down refugee from a Goodwill Center. Only more thread-bare. "I had that one suit to my name. Believe me, that's all I had. I would take the coat off and I would wear a shirt and tie to class. I scooted back and forth on those seats up there until the pants were so thin. I'm not kidding you. I was afraid to stoop over." Anyone forced to take Latin in high school will surely remember the famous phrase, "Vestis virum reddit." Translated it means, "Clothes make the man." It certainly didn't apply to Preacher. When the final grades were posted, Preacher had successfully completed the first year of the formal training required to become licensed as a Christian & Missionary Alliance preacher. And he had two As and eight Bs on his transcript to prove it.

Chapter 11

Pack Up The Kids

"For God so loved the world that He gave His only begotten Son, that whosoever believeth on Him should not perish but have everlasting life." **John 3:16 (NIV)**

Once back from Nyack, Preacher was grateful to have his old job back as a welder in the coal mine for the summer months. He made it a practice to read his New Testament during lunch hour and to witness to anyone who would listen about the goodness of the Lord. One of these miners who did show an interest, Billy Reed, stopped by Preacher's welding booth on several occasions and asked him about the Bible. Then one day, during his lunch break, Reed asked Preacher about salvation. It was the opening Preacher had been praying for. Preacher told Reed how much God loved him and how anxious He was for him to become a part of the family of God. He then shared the plan of salvation and read several scriptures from the New Testament. Preacher explained that the "whosoever" meant him, Billy Reed. They knelt there in the mining camp and Reed accepted Jesus as his personal Savior. Preacher could hardly wait to get home and tell Freda what had happened that day at work. Freda recalled later that a great peace came over her as she listened. "There was do doubt that we were in God's will. That's why I can't understand kids that go away to Bible School and have no idea why they are there. I think that's why we have the ministry now as a profession, not a calling."

Over the next few weeks Preacher and Freda prayed about his second year at Nyack, asking the Lord to provide a way where she and the three children could be with him. And sure enough, within a couple of days a letter from Nyack came offering Preacher the job of apartment manager for Bissell Hall which was used for married couples. For managing the four-apartment building, Preacher and his family would be able to live there rent free.

Preacher continued to work at the mine that summer of 1945 and continued to witness for the Lord. He and Freda also started tying up lose ends and making plans to move the entire family to Nyack. Freda resigned her job at Westinghouse and Preacher said goodbye to his friends and co-workers at the mine. Once again they passed the hat around and gave Preacher money to help with his expenses for the second year. Some if not most of the men who donated money were not Christians. That was the kind of impact Preacher had on people's lives. Although Preacher's father thought it was a mistake for him to return to Nyack — and told him that in no uncertain times — he agreed to take the family back in his car since they couldn't afford the train fare.

Talk about hate at first sight. Whey they got to Nyack and drove up to Bissell Hall,

Freda recalled thinking to herself she had never seen anything as ugly as that big old building. It had already been condemned and it was just a matter of time before they would have to raze it to the ground — or at least what hadn't fallen down already. The inside was even worse. Preacher had been assigned the middle apartment, and when they walked down the hall and opened the door, Freda just shook her head. The walls were corrugated tin and painted a battleship gray. "The only thing I remember is I shut the door and turned around and told June, 'Let's go home.' My initiation to Nyack. I thought, I can't handle this. I didn't question God, but..." School would be starting in a few days and another chapter in their lives was about to begin.

Chapter 12

God Does Provide

"For every animal of the forest is mine. And the cattle on a Thousand Hills."
Psalm 50:10 (NIV)

After Preacher and Freda moved what little furniture they owned into the apartment, one thing in particular became very apparent. There was only one bedroom and it wasn't very big. Scrounging around in the basement of the building, they found an old set of bunk beds for Jim and Earl, putting them in the bedroom with their own bed. Preacher, Freda and the boys would sleep there, while Barbara would have to spend nights on the couch in the living room. Their only furniture consisted of a living room chair, baby grand piano and kitchen table and chairs. As they carefully "arranged" the table in the kitchen, Preacher wondered to himself how they would ever keep food on it — if, of course, they figured out a way to afford any. "The floors in the apartment were so rickety that we had to put wedges under the table to make it level enough to keep milk in the bowls." The only bright spot in the apartment was the piano that had been the pride and joy of Preacher's mother, Mahalia. She had made it known she wanted Barbara to have the piano when she died. It was the only material item they owned that had any value.

As the apartment manager, Preacher and Freda ordered the milk for all the tenants, collecting the money at the end of each month. In return, the Freelands were given a free quart of milk each day — not much for a family of five. Although Preacher volunteered for every odd job he heard about, there never seemed to be enough money to make ends meet. "The people downtown would call for someone to cut their lawn or do other handyman jobs. The would announce it in chapel and my hand was always up." There were times when he didn't know where the next loaf of bread would come from. "Not only the next loaf, the next slice," he recalled. "They would call sometimes from the cafeteria kitchen where the single students ate and say there were some beans or something left over if we would bring a bowl down. I tell you, I always had a big pan ready."

Preacher was pleased when he received his course curriculum for the second year. There was the study of Acts, Hebrews and the Poetical Books, along with Alliance Doctrine, Biblical Theology, Evangelism and Homiletics. The only subject he dreaded was English, and he was going to have to take it both semesters.

Although times were certainly tough, it never crossed Preacher's mind to give up. It seemed like every time he started feeling sorry for himself God would make Himself known in a special way. One day he was walking back to the apartment, dirty in his work clothes from an afternoon of cutting lawns, when a man walked up beside him and started talking about his rich brother. The man said his brother lived upstate and owned a bunch of cows. Preacher listened for a few minutes and, although dead tired and filthy, decided to witness to the man. "I'm a rich man, too." The man stopped and looked at Preacher quizzically. Preacher continued, "Yeah, my heavenly Father owns the cattle on a thousand hills and all the gold and silver, and I am one of His heirs." Preacher would never forget the look on the man's face. God had once again reminded him of his worth.

By the time October rolled around the Freeland family had settled into a routine of sorts. Freda had started working at the five-and-dime store downtown and Barbara and Jim were in school. Preacher was enjoying his classes, particularly the extra assignments that included speaking at nearby Alliance churches. His favorite one was the Bergen Street Alliance Church in Brooklyn. One of the students at Nyack, Ed Smiley, had grown up in the church and his parents were regular members. A week or so before Thanksgiving, Preacher was asked to preach at Bergen Street and after the Sunday service he along with the entire Smiley family went out to lunch.

On the afternoon before Thanksgiving, Preacher was sitting in his chair studying when Jim bounced into the room after returning from school. The kids in his class had been talking about the turkey dinner they would feast on the next day. Climbing into Preacher's lap, Jim asked, "Dad, are we going to have a turkey for Thanksgiving?" Preacher and Freda had saved just enough money to have some hamburger so he told Jim, "No Buddy, I don't think so." Preacher's heart broke when he saw the disappointment on his son's face. As they were sitting there, the mailman delivered a letter from Ed Smiley's parents containing a crisp five-dollar bill. "That was a lot of money. I told Jimmy to get his coat on, we were going downtown. We went to a little store we dealt with and I told the man I wanted that turkey right there. It was four dollars and something. He didn't have a piece of paper big enough to wrap it in and its legs were hanging out." Preacher and Jim then marched right over to the five-and-dime store and showed it to Freda. They stood in the middle of the store and cried a river of joy. They even took a picture of the turkey and for years smiled whenever they looked at it.

Although Nyack conducted Sunday morning services on campus, Preacher and his family usually attended the Alliance church in town. For two good reasons. The first Sunday there, the Freelands attended the on-campus service to hear the president of Nyack speak. Freda remembered the president addressing the students and reminding them that, although they might have had a big job in their home churches, here they were starting on the bottom rung of the ladder. "In other words," Freda recounted, "go back to your room and be quiet." The next time they attended the on-campus service was when the school choir performed *"Handel's Messiah"* during the Christmas season. When they arrived at the auditorium, the only seats left were up near the front. The program had already started, and Dr. Olson, resplendent in his black tuxedo with tails, led a rousing rendition of the first part of the 1741 classic. During intermission, Dr. Olson, a magnificently dignified man, sat down on the seat right in front of the Freelands. When he got back up to begin the second part of the program Freda noticed something on the tails of his tuxedo. "When he got up there, on the tails of the back of his coat were Earl's two little footprints. Sand." Preacher never had the nerve to tell him." After that, Preacher figured it was safer if they just made the two-mile walk into town on Sundays.

Another remarkable thing happened during that Christmas season. The Lord sent new clothes for Freda and the children. Again, it was Ed Smiley's parents who allowed Him to use them. And knowing that no Christmas would be complete without presents, they had also stuffed toys in the clothing for Barbara, Jim and Earl.

Later that winter Jim got a cold that kept getting worse by the day. Although they had no health insurance, Preacher had a doctor come to the apartment. After examining him, the doctor told Preacher that Jim had pneumonia and would need to be taken to the hospital. Knowing they could not pay a hospital bill, Preacher told the doctor they would keep him home that night and see how he was doing the next morning. As soon as the doctor left, Preacher called the college to have the students pray for Jim. He and Freda got down on their knees and started doing the same. The next morning, when the doctor showed up, not only was the fever gone but there were no signs he had even been sick. The doctor was amazed and told Preacher he had come with every intention of insisting they put Jim in the hospital. Although the doctor couldn't understand what had happened, Preacher and Freda sure could. God had heard the prayers and completely healed their son.

Preacher felt pretty proud of himself when he got his grades for the first semester. With the exception of a C+ in English, he had managed to get all As and Bs. He had done well in all of his Bible courses, and he felt like he was making progress when it came to speaking in front of an audience. Part of his curriculum required that he spend a few evenings and weekends witnessing to strangers in the streets of New York City. Preacher loved this course requirement along with occasionally preaching at a nearby church. His first opportunity to prepare a sermon and preach it to other Nyack students came in late March 1946 as an assignment in his Homiletics class. A few days after preaching the sermon, a character study of Nehemiah, his professor, Gilbert H. Johnson, wrote him a letter. In it he reminded Preacher to be careful with his pronouns and he brought up a few enunciation suggestions. But over all, he was more than complimentary. Excerpted from the letter, he wrote: "We are all blessed when we listen to you preach because we know it is coming from a sincere heart and that you have a real desire to be at your best always for the Lord... On the whole you did a fine piece of work and I know that as you continue to work diligently along the line of preaching, God will have an important ministry for you in the days to come. Stick to it, my brother, it pays real dividends."

Although Johnson was probably the strictest professor at Nyack, Preacher loved to sit under his teaching. He encouraged Preacher almost daily and repeatedly reminded him to always trust in the Lord. If he couldn't do that, he should just go back home. Preacher had no problem with the trusting part. He had seen God work in his life many times and knew it was only through His grace that he was surviving at Nyack. "God not only brings guys like me to schools to prepare for His work, He has instruments like Mr. Johnson in place to help us grow."

As spring edged out winter, Preacher was able to get more part-time jobs in town. But making ends meet was still a daily battle. His one pair of dress pants were becoming thinner by the day. "The seat was so thin you could read a newspaper through them." One day a call came in at school that a Jewish lawyer in town by the name of Sol needed his yard cut. Preacher got the job. After he had finished mowing and cleaning up, Preacher and Sol walked around inspecting the job. During the conversation, the lawyer asked Preacher what he was doing at Nyack. He told him the Lord had called him to be a pastor. They chatted for a few more minutes and after paying Preacher, Sol invited him into his house. "I walked into this Jewish lawyer's house and he took me into a room with a big closet. He took this coat out and said 'try it on.' It fit me perfectly. He then had me try on the pants to the suit. They fit like they had been tailored for me. He gave me three suits that day and six white shirts to go with them — lawyer suits and shirts. I walked out of the room with suits and shirts under my arms and tears running down my face." Those three suits and six shirts carried Preacher through college and well into his first pastorate. Suddenly he was the best-dressed student on campus.

A few weeks later Sol called Preacher and asked if he knew anything about plumbing. He had a camper in the Catskill Mountains and wanted to run a line to a hot-water heater. Preacher told him he had been a welder and had a classmate who knew a little something about pipes, tanks, fittings and such. The next Saturday, the lawyer drove Preacher and his classmate, Clyde Dearmette, to the camp. "My buddy was about as dumb as I was but we were both married and needed the money." They started running the pipe to the hot-water heater and got about half the job done, stopping only for lunch. They returned the next two Saturdays to finish the job. At lunch the first two weekends, Preacher thanked the Lord for the food. But on the third Saturday, Sol insisted he give the thanks and prayed a Jewish prayer. Preacher never saw the man again, but often thanked the Lord for sending him in a time of need.

As the end of the school year approached, Preacher prepared for semester exams. He also decided his family would spend the summer at Nyack. When the final grades were posted, Preacher could hardly believe what he saw — all were Bs, including a B+ in English. Two years down and only one to go.

Chapter 13

One More Year

"Preach the Word, be prepared in season and out of season; correct, rebuke and encourage — with great patience and careful instruction." **2 Timothy 4:2 (NIV)**

The summer of 1946 was a busy one for Preacher and Freda. They remained on campus and were able to move into Wilson Hall, a much nicer apartment. Again, Preacher and Freda were going to manage the building, meaning they would be assured of at least a quart of milk each day. And both Preacher and Freda were able to get on-campus summer jobs. Preacher was hired as a painter and Freda as a secretary for the school, a job she would keep through Preacher's graduation. Barbara was 11 years old by now and able to watch Jim and Earl while her parents were at work. By the time the fall semester rolled around, Preacher was wondering what his last year at Nyack would be like and more importantly, what plans God had for his future.

Right before the new school year began, Preacher landed a job driving a public school bus. Since he would be required to work afternoons, he scheduled all his classes for the morning. During his final year he was required to complete studies including Church History, Christ in the Bible, Isaiah, Jeremiah, Ephesians, Theology, Biblical Theology, Christian Evidences, Pastoral Methods, Highlights in Missions, Survey of Christian Education, Homiletics II and Church Music. Although no such class was offered, Preacher wished they would have included one on how to pass all those subjects, drive a school bus full of kids every day and raise a family of three children all at the same time.

Although Preacher knew he had been called into the ministry, he started to wonder exactly what path he was supposed to follow. During his first year he had read the book Mother India and joined the India prayer group on campus. He had a real interest in the missionary program of his denomination and felt like the Lord might be leading him towards becoming a Christian & Missionary Alliance missionary. He had also recently been appointed by the school's president, Dr. Mosely, as president of the Friday Night Missionary Service — the highest honor a student could receive at Nyack. Certain he was doing the right thing, he applied to become a missionary. Preacher was unable to hide his disappointment when his application was rejected because of his age and the fact he had three children. Freda encouraged Preacher and reminded him that all they ever wanted was to be in His will. "If you really want to do God's will, you just do it. It becomes contagious. There are no disappointments if you're working with God. Put that in your book. Another thing, I never ask God why. If God is God, I'm sand on a scale. If I give Him my life, I have to believe He will take care of me."

Classes were going great for Preacher. As he studied with other students, he was amazed at just how much he had learned about the Bible. And how he enjoyed assignments where he was able to speak in different churches or go into town and witness on the streets. It was obvious to his professors and classmates that he had a special gift for relating to people, especially young ones. His Homiletics professor, Gilbert Johnson, was particularly impressed. Sometime during that final year, he visited Preacher and Freda to offer words of encouragement. Admitting that he had been hard on Preacher during his classes, Johnson told them he saw something special in him. Freda recalled Johnson saying that if he had to "put all of my eggs in one basket" he believed Preacher would most likely succeed in preaching the Gospel in such a way that men and women would want to know Jesus as their personal Savior.

Driving the public school bus turned out to be real adventure for Preacher. "I don't know how many kids I was able to lead to the Lord while driving that bus. These were public school kids. I would talk to them about the Lord. As we neared the end of the line there would be fewer kids on board and I would have more time to talk to them on a personal level. The Lord just kept on putting opportunities in front of me. Doors kept opening." Preacher had a good voice and loved to sing, and he would teach the kids all the Christian songs and choruses he knew. Out of the blue he would start a song and one by one the kids would join in. By the end of the school year, they would beg Preacher to drive slower so they would have more time to sing.

At home, the Freelands were discovering that Barbara was musically gifted, just like Preacher's mom had been. A student at Nyack, Gilbert Sisio, was an accomplished pianist and had been giving Barbara lessons in exchange for Freda doing his laundry. It didn't take long for him realize Barbara had an unusual talent for tickling the ivories. Although she could have become a concert pianist, Barbara used those talents instead to glorify her Lord her entire life.

With the school year almost over, Preacher still had no idea what he would be doing after graduation. One of his classmates was from Union City, PA, and was a member of the Alliance church there. The church was very small and had just lost its pastor because of moral issues. Talk was that the denomination was about ready to close it. The student, during a visit home, mentioned to the church board that he knew an older student at Nyack who was graduating and probably looking for a church to pastor. After the church board talked to the district superintendent, Preacher was contacted and asked to candidate for the position of pastor of the Union City Christian & Missionary Alliance Church.

The next Sunday Preacher and Freda rode the train to Union City. Before leaving, they prayed that God would go with them and show them His will. The church had been without a pastor for a while and attendance had declined to about 35 regulars. However, the Sunday morning he candidated there, about 75 people showed up. He delivered both the morning and evening sermons and five people accepted Christ. Scheduled to return to Nyack the next day, Preacher met with the church board Monday morning and, before he and Freda could even get on the train back, was offered the position. Preacher accepted the call right there, agreeing to be their pastor upon graduation. Freda was so excited. "He said yes, I don't have any place else to go. We were just looking for a door to open and there it was. I guess they couldn't get anyone else to candidate. He didn't even discuss salary. It was all free-will giving."

A couple of weeks before graduation, Preacher spoke at a church in upstate New York and afterwards was invited to a member's house for lunch. When asked what he planned to do, Preacher told the man about his call to Union City. When asked how he was going to get his family there, Preacher shook his head and said he had no idea. The man then told Preacher he had an old Chevrolet in his garage and would sell it to him for $360. Preacher knew the car was worth more than that but he didn't even have three dollars and thirty-six cents in his pocket. He thanked him and said he would love to have the car but just couldn't afford it.

The week before graduation, Preacher went home to West Virginia for a couple of days. There was no special reason for him to go, but he just felt the Lord was telling him to do so. "I went to the shop at the mine to see some guys I knew. Hard hats and black faces. We were talking about my schooling and I told them what I was going to do. I started to leave and they asked me to stick around for a little longer. I messed around until the whistle blew and these guys started gathering around me. One of the guys reached into his pocket and pulled out a wad of bills. Preacher remembered him saying, "We know you're graduating and we wanted to give you this money as a graduation present." When Preacher counted the money, it was to the dollar what the car cost.

Preacher went straight to upstate New York, paid for the car and headed back to school. The tires were dry-rotted and he had to stop three or four times for repairs. When he finally got to the town of Nyack he pulled into a gasoline station owned by Gus Gleeson. Although they were not close friends, Preacher had watched the station for Gleeson a couple of times and spoke in his church on one occasion. As they talked, Gleeson asked Preacher where he was going. After answering "Not far [in this car]," Preacher told him the Lord had called him to Union City and after graduation he and his family were packing up and heading for his first pastorate. Saying he had a quick errand to run, Gleeson asked Preacher if he would mind watching the gas station while he was gone. He agreed, and while waiting for Gleeson to get back, Preacher started thinking about how he was going to make it to Union City with those four bald tires. Although the war had ended, it was still next to impossible to buy tires — even if he had the money. After about 45 minutes, Gleeson returned in his truck and off-loaded four brand-new tires. "He put them on my car and wouldn't take a penny. He said this is my contribution to your ministry. I was so overwhelmed I could hardly say thank you." God had provided yet

[55]

another miracle.

Graduation night finally arrived. To his surprise, Preacher's dad and stepmother, along with his Uncle Howard and his wife, showed up totally unannounced. Preacher's dad and stepmother were not Christians and had taken little or no interest in him while he was at Nyack. In fact, they had never sent he or the children a single penny the entire three years. Although he didn't know much about Uncle Howard, he had heard he was part of the Baltimore Colts football organization and owned a chain of steakhouses. Later that night he gave Preacher a football signed by Colts' players and a fresh $20 dollar bill for his graduation.

Preacher was one of four graduates asked to speak that evening and he chose the Lordship of Jesus Christ as his topic. It was the perfect subject for a man who had trusted God to see him through his three years at Nyack. A review of his final college transcript revealed Preacher had received a total of 11 As, 26 Bs and one C. Not bad for a West Virginian coal miner.

Chapter 14

Union City — Learning To Lean On God

"The Lord will guide you always; He will satisfy your needs in a sun-scorched land and will strengthen your frame." **Isaiah 58:11 (NIV)**

There's an old saying by experienced pastors Preacher learned at Nyack that goes, "Beware of the guy who meets you at the train." Preacher and his family arrived in Union City, PA, the first week in June 1947. And while they arrived in his old Chevrolet and not by steel horse, those words turned out to be prophetic. Arriving with a stomach full of butterflies, Preacher was met by the Sunday School superintendent, Mr. King. Although always in love, Mr. King would give Preacher a harder time than anyone else during his tenure as pastor at Union City Alliance Church. After showing Preacher the church, Mr. King took the family to the parsonage they were to call home. Mr. King also informed Preacher that the church had only rented it for six months. Not exactly the vote of confidence Preacher was looking for.

Licensed to preach but not yet ordained, Preacher delivered his first sermon at Union City on June 8. He spent the two or three days leading up to it trying to put a sermon together, but found himself spending even more time wondering if he was ready to be a full-time pastor. "I was worried if I could fill the bill... prepare three or four sermons a week. There was a lot of anticipation." Looking over the empty pews among the 30 or so worshippers that day, Preacher began asking the Lord to help him be the kind of shepherd they so desperately needed. After the morning and evening services were over, Preacher felt an abiding peace come over him and knew he was in God's will.

The church paid the rent for the parsonage and the utility bills. Preacher and his family lived on whatever free-will offering was put into the collection plate. Tithe offerings went toward the expenses of operating the church. Preacher's "salary" that first Sunday was $17 and would sometimes be as little as $12.

Still, Freda was amazed at the way God answered their prayers. At the beginning of the week she would list their needs and take them to the Lord in prayer. "Lord, You know these are our needs and You know this is what we have," she would pray. She remembered "reminding" the Lord she had three kids and no washing machine... and within a week there was one in her basement. Sometimes she would get a letter from as far away as 400 miles from a friend. One said, "I was washing dishes and the Lord told me you needed help. It was so urgent I stopped and wrote you this check." It would be for the exact amount they needed. Preacher and her witnessed the answer to prayer over and over as they trusted in Him.

Preacher looked back at that first Sunday in Union City. "I was so scared I didn't know up from down. One thing, though, the church really grew that first Sunday. Me and Freda and the three kids." From the beginning, the Lord blessed the church. Young couples and families started attending and souls were being saved. There was a sense of excitement as the church grew.

After they had been at Union City for six months, the folks who owned the parsonage decided to sell it. Preacher and the church started praying about what to do. Even though the church owned a parcel of land next to the church large enough for a parsonage, there was no money in the treasury to build it. Preacher was in the local barber shop talking to some of the guys about this dilemma. One of them piped in, "Hey, I've got a bulldozer and I'll come over and dig your foundation for thirty-five dollars." It didn't take long for the church to catch the vision. Austin Peterson, a church board member, had befriended Preacher when it looked like his old Chevrolet was going to sit down like a camel in the middle of the dessert. Peterson arranged for Preacher to get a "newer" old car and was even making all the payments. Hearing about the offer of the bulldozer, Peterson said, "I've got a farm with a lot of maple trees on it. You know how hard maple is to nail. If you guys want to come cut the trees down, I've got enough maple to build a parsonage."

The church had a tree-cutting day out at Peterson's farm and the logs were taken to a nearby hopper mill where they were turned into two-by-fours and other needed sizes. While the wood was drying, the basement was dug and foundation laid. Church member Jan Morvay was a master carpenter and volunteered to the be the foreman on the job. Morvay had tuberculosis as a chid and one of his arms was shorter than the other. Nevertheless, Preacher had never seen anyone work as hard or as long as he did. "As I look back, Jan and I would work when is was so cold you could hardly drive a nail. We did most of the work on the parsonage. I have no idea how many hours he donated." In addition to the maple trees, Peterson had allowed enough cherry trees on his property to be cut down to panel the study in the parsonage. That cherry-paneled study was the most beautiful room Preacher had ever seen and he spent countless hours there preparing sermons and reflecting on His goodness. Because of a lack of money, the only thing left unfinished was the basement so it was on a dirt floor that Freda did the laundry.

The little Alliance church in Union City continued to grow in numbers. Preacher was learning early on the importance of making himself available to the community. He became a regular at the barber shop. Or he would go into the department store and buy a cheap handkerchief just so he could talk to the salesperson about the Lord. Preacher believed, "That ought to be the norm, not anything extra. It ought to be natural that we want to share what the Lord has done for us." Preacher was always sharing his testimony. One day early in his ministry in Union City, Preacher met an older, white-haired man named Dave on the street. After greeting him, Preacher asked Dave where he was going on such a beautiful day. "Well, I reckon I'm on my way to Hell eventually, but right now I'm on my way to the store." That day preacher led Dave to the Lord and a new name was written down in Glory.

Among Preacher's early converts was George Cooper and his wife. She started attending the church alone and found the Lord. The Coopers owned a family grocery store, so Preacher started stopping by there just to buy a pack of chewing gum — again, anything to get the opportunity to talk to Mr. Cooper about his Savior. Eventually he came to church with his wife and accepted the Lord. After his conversion, Cooper went back to his little grocery store and got himself some Gospel tracts. From then on, every bag of groceries that left the store contained God's plan for salvation. And it didn't stop there. Cooper started witnessing to his customers. Preacher smiled when he remembered the "teamwork" he and Cooper developed. "Every once in a while he would call me and ask me to come on down to the store because he had a guy in the back room. I know three or four people who came to know the Lord in that back room. George would witness to them and would call me to lead them to the Lord." Although he was a young Christian and didn't know much about the scriptures, Cooper knew that souls were important. So Cooper led the "team" in wins while Preacher piled up the saves.

Cooper also took another huge step in faith. He cleaned out his store of all cigarettes, cigars and chewing tobacco. People told him he would lose his business and some of his regular customers threatened to quit shopping in his store. His only response was the Lord would send new people in. And He did. Not too long after that, his brother and sister-in-law also accepted the Lord and became a part of the Union City church.

Although God was blessing the church those first few months, some folks in the little town of a couple thousand were skeptical if it would last. The previous pastor had been asked to leave and everybody knew the details of his dismissal. Preacher would walk down the street and notice people avoiding him. That only made him more determined to witness to anyone he came in contact with and show them God's love. Moe Robertson, a Jewish store owner, was one of those people. Preacher would often go into Robertson's store just to say hello. Although he was never able to lead him to the Lord, Preacher and Robertson had some great talks. It was around 1948 and many Jews were returning to Israel and Jerusalem in particular. During one of their conversations, Robertson looked Preacher in the eye and confessed that if he were younger he'd leave that day and move back "home." Something was drawing him. Robertson and Preacher became close friends the five years he was in Union City.

And so the pattern continued. One by one, the Lord led Preacher to new friends. One of these was Dr. Picutt, who was the chairman of an organization that included veterinarians throughout Pennsylvania. Doctor Picutt's next-door neighbors had gotten saved and joined the Alliance church. One Sunday they invited Mrs. Picutt to a service and she accepted Christ that day, opening the door to a friendship between Preacher and her husband. Sometimes he would invite Preacher to observe an interesting operation he was performing. Other times he would invite Preacher to a dinner of lobster or some other fancy meal. "That was something, a guy like me making nineteen dollars a week eating lobster." And a couple of times Dr. Picutt took Preacher with him on fishing trips to Canada. Doctor Picutt owned a cabin on a bay eight miles from the nearest paved road and they would fish on a lake so clear you could see the bottom. "We would catch those fish, build a fire and have a fish fry right there. They can't get any fresher than that."

It was while visiting Dr. Picutt's hunting camp that Preacher fell in love with deer hunting. Knowing absolutely nothing about the sport, he announced the first morning he went that he would get himself a big one. Doctor Picutt just laughed and told Preacher that if he shot anything over a four-pointer, he would have the buck mounted for him. And wouldn't you know it... "This deer came up over the hill flying. I followed him down and shot him. He was eight-point buck. I was so dumb I pulled that deer all the way back to camp without cleaning him out. I didn't know you were supposed to do that. I really got some ribbing over that." That deer would hang in a prominent place in Preacher's den the rest of his life.

Freda was in the basement one day doing the laundry when Dr. Picutt stopped by. When he saw the dirt floor he asked Freda why there was no concrete. He then went and found Preacher and told him Freda shouldn't be doing his laundry in a mud hole. A few days later Dr. Picutt had a contractor pour the floor for the basement. The parsonage was now complete and totally debt free. At about the same time they were pouring the concrete, Earl broke his leg. One day, while the cement mixer was still in the yard, Preacher looked out and Earl was standing on top of it cast and all. If that wasn't enough, the next day he saw his son riding his bicycle down the road peddling with just his one good leg. Although he was busy being the pastor of a growing church, Preacher always took time for his children. One of Earl's fondest memories was the first time his dad took him pheasant hunting. Earl was just five years old and as they were walking through a cornfield with the sun in their eyes, a bird flew up. With the accuracy of a Daniel Boone, Preacher shot the bird dead. But there was one problem. You were only allowed to shoot male pheasants, or what they called Ring necks, and the bird Preacher had shot was a hen. Earl remembered his dad going straight home and calling the game warden. "This was at dad's first pastorate and he was making maybe twelve dollars a week. When the game warden came, the fine was just about one week's salary and he took the bird. As the game warden was leaving he turned and said he was supposed to take the bird and give it to the poor. So he handed the bird back to dad and said, 'You are the poorest people I know.'"

Preacher's oldest son, Jim, had his own story to tell. The first year they were in Union City, both him and Earl got red boxing gloves for Christmas. Jim was seven at the time, two years older than Earl. Both of them were so excited that they immediately put the gloves on. Both had already developed a competitive spirit, and within a few short minutes, were knocking the stuffing out each other. So Preacher stepped in and said it was time he teach both of them some lessons in the fine art of boxing. Putting on Earl's gloves and tying them up good and tight, he got on his knees so that he would be about the same height as Jim. He then showed Jim how to hold his fists and arms just right so he could block punches. He then announced he was going to show Jim exactly how it was supposed to be done, instructing his oldest son to give him his best shot. He did just that. "I wound up and hit dad with my best haymaker, right in the nose. Blood flew everywhere. He was yelling for mom to get him a wash rag. The last thing I saw was him staggering out through the archway to the kitchen, holding a wet towel over his nose. That's the last boxing lesson I ever remember."

On January 25, 1948, a little over six months after arriving in Union City, Preacher and Freda were blessed with their last child, Bob. He was born in a house that had been converted into a hospital. Their family was now complete.

As the months rolled by, Preacher developed a style and tone of ministry that would follow him throughout his "career." His Sunday morning service was usually geared to evangelism, since he felt there would be more unsaved people in the audience. He strongly believed that feeding the flock was paramount, and the only way to know the needs of his congregation was to become a part of their lives. And while weddings, visitation, counseling and a myriad of other responsibilities were important to him, his passion was seeing souls won into the Kingdom of God. Hence, he never preached a sermon without giving an invitation at the end, always feeling that the Lord might have spoken to someone.

As he matured as a young paster he realized that preparation was critical. "You have to build a file with illustrations for different special occasions. When you're working on a theme, God lays it on your heart but doesn't do your research for you. Rely on your experiences. Read. Study yourself full and preach yourself empty. The larger the church the less you have to study." Still good advice for any of you future pastors out there.

Another dynamic started to work in the Union City Alliance Church — music. Preacher always made singing an integral part of his services. After learning that one of his members played the saxophone and another, George Cooper, played the trombone, Preacher started a mini-orchestra and incorporated it into the program. Jim was taking trumpet lessons in school and became part of that group. It was a novelty of sorts back then to have instruments other than the standard organ and piano in church, and some people came just to hear the group play. It wasn't long before Union City Alliance became known as the church with the great music.

Another unexpected turn of events impacted the Freeland family during their ministry in Union City. Preacher's sister, Babe, and her husband and two children moved into town right next door. The entire family was unsaved and Babe was often abused both mentally and physically by her husband. Preacher led Babe to the Lord and shortly after that her husband left her. Babe would go on to serve the Lord the rest of her life.

As a young pastor, the most difficult task for Preacher was conducting funerals — especially if they were friends or, much worse, non-believers. He remembered one of the hardest being a little girl who he had prayed for when she was sick. Standing in the wet, cold snow with her parents as they lowered the little white coffin into the ground nearly broke his heart, and for a long time Preacher and the girl's parents stood there and cried. Later, Preacher was able to lead both of them to the Lord and took comfort in the fact that one day they would be reunited with their baby girl. "Every funeral is hard. Sometimes the knowledge that they knew the Lord was what got me through."

Preacher had already seen his son, Jim, healed of pneumonia while at Nyack, so praying for the sick was a natural part of his ministry. Jan Morvay, who had been so instrumental in building the parsonage, had a three-year-old son who became very ill and was not expected to live. Preacher went to visit the child in the hospital and was told by the nurse that the boy was having an especially bad day and had just gone to sleep. Preacher explained to her the Lord had sent him to pray for the boy, so he laid his hand on him and poured out his heart to God. "That was one of those special times when the whole world seemed to be filled with the glory of the Lord. You could sense it as if He was standing there. I finished praying and he never moved. The nurse told me I must have the touch." The Lord healed Morvay's son that very day and he returned home the next week.

It was while pastoring at Union City that Preacher and Freda began the practice of inviting different families home with them for cake and coffee after Sunday evening service. On one occasion, the five-year-old son of the visiting family was asked to say the blessing. Giving it his best effort, the boy prayed around the world for what seemed like hours. Preacher's daughter, Barbara, remembered how happy she was when the boy seemingly had exhausted all his prayer know-how. Just when they thought he was finished, he blurted out, "... and h-h-h-h-help me Lord, I don't like my dog." The prayer ended with everyone around the table bursting out in laughter. That incident would be recounted many times at Freeland family gatherings.

Since they didn't own a television set or anything like that, the Freelands would often pile into the old black Chevy sedan and go out for an ice cream cone. With no air-conditioning or radio, they would chug along with all the windows down singing as loud as they could. The family had a lot of fun on those evenings singing everything from *"Row, Row, Row Your Boat"* to *"Amazing Grace"* and any other song that would come to mind. Or they would just make up a song on the fly. When they would come to a stoplight, Barbara would crouch down on the floorboard so no one could see she was part of that crazy Freeland family.

But the music wasn't just confined to the car. Many evenings after supper, Barbara would sit down at the piano and begin playing. It wouldn't take long for Jim to join in with his trumpet. Earl, who had just started taking music lessons at school, would get into the mix next with his trombone. Barbara fondly remembered these special times. "Pretty soon we would hear Dad going upstairs and we knew what was going to happen — he was going to join in with his saxophone or mandolin. Well, if it was his mandolin, we would continue with our impromptu concert. But if he brought down the saxophone, one by one we each of us would suddenly have something extremely pressing that could only be done right then."

Jim, too, remembered how much he enjoyed the after-supper music sessions. "We were loud and we were good. One of our favorite songs was "When the Saints Go Marching In." I remember one summer night we forgot to close the windows before we started. About halfway through our hoedown, one of our neighbors walked over, reached in from the outside, and closed the windows for us... great memories."

Somehow Preacher also found time to coach a youth baseball team while in Union City. Most of his players were boys from the church. Jim was the shortstop and Earl the catcher, and they both made the all-star team in the eight to 12-year-old league. It was the beginning of very promising teenage careers for both of them.

By the summer of 1950, the Alliance church in Union City was nearly busting at the seams. The Sunday School was averaging between 125 and 150 attendees each week, and people were being saved on a regular basis. Preacher had been there almost three years before the district superintendent paid him his first visit and asked how things were going. "I told him pretty good, gave him the statistics and told him how people were being saved. He looked at me funny and told me he had come to close the church. I told him he'd better throw the padlock away, 'cause we're moving on for the Lord.'"

Preacher did not hear back from the district superintendent until nearly a year later. When he did, it was to ask Preacher if he would be willing to candidate at a small Alliance church about two hours away in western Pennsylvania. Although he was not looking to move, he said "yes." When Preacher told Freda of his decision, she agreed without hesitation. God had laid it on her heart that their time in Union City was coming to a close. "We never put our name on a list to candidate in our ministry. We never talked to each other about it being time to move. God would talk to each one of us individually. He would then open the door. We felt if we did the choosing, it wouldn't be His will. If He did the choosing, we couldn't fail."

As he traveled to Bradford, PA, to candidate that weekend, Preacher already knew in his heart that he and his family would be packing up.

Chapter 15

I Love To Hunt

"Jesus said, 'Let the little children come to me, and do not hinder them, for the Kingdom of heaven belongs to such as these." **Matthew 19:14 (NIV)**

The Bradford Alliance Church was located about 90 miles from Union City, PA. The church was smaller than the one he was currently pastoring, but Preacher had the feeling he would be called there. The previous pastor had already resigned to take another church and three other candidates had been interviewed. After preaching that Sunday morning, Preacher was given a quick tour. The church and parsonage were connected and located by the railroad tracks in a run-down part of town. That night, after his sermon, the church board unanimously called him to be their pastor.

Although it was a step down if that was possible, Preacher was sure it was the Lord's will and accepted the position right away. Later, as he and Freda prayed about it, they both had the same sense they would not be in Bradford very long. It was a strange move on paper, but they knew it was what God wanted. Preacher gave the Union City Alliance Church three weeks notice and started packing up. None of his children complained about moving and on a cold winter morning, Preacher and his family closed another chapter in their lives.

As he had done in Union City, Preacher made it a point to meet as many people in Bradford as possible. Before long, he was widely known as the Alliance preacher who was a true friend to everyone, especially the children. He was never too busy to spend time with young people, always teasing them good-heartily and taking time to really listen to what they had to say. Still, Preacher found it hard to break down all the barriers. People came to know the Lord while he was in Bradford, but not like he wanted. One who did was Mrs. Day. The wife of a grocer, she came to know the Lord under Preacher's ministry and, in her job cleaning houses, went on to witness to dozens of people.

One of the many downsides about Bradford was a lack of a place for his children to play. Preacher lost count of how many windows he had to replace in the garage next to the parsonage. So instead, whenever he could, Preacher would take his oldest son, Jim, hunting. Preacher remembered "Buying hand-warmers and gloves, long underwear, boots, shells, hunting licenses and many other things too numerous to mention. We figured one year if we took all the money we spent and divided by the pounds of meat we got, the meat cost us about forty-two dollars a pound." But Preacher and Jim didn't mind, because it was worth it just to see Freda's happy face when they brought home their catch. One of Jim's happiest birthdays was his

12th when Preacher bought him his very own 410-gauge shotgun. Later on, Earl and Bob would get the same birthday present when they turned 12.

One cold winter morning Preacher and Jim went deer hunting. If there had been anything like a Bass Pro Shop back then, they would have been the poster children for it. In addition to their hunting gear, they took with them snacks and a big lunch they planned to cook over Sterno canned heat. Sitting together in the woods watching for deer, they had a blanket over their laps with a can of the Sterno underneath to keep warm. Smelling something, Preacher lifted the blanket to find that Jim had burned a hole right through the good pair of corduroy pants he had on. They laughed and laughed. Until they had to go home and tell Freda what had happened.

While in Bradford, Barbara got her first paying job in a shoe store. She spent some of her money on new clothes, a far cry from the hand-me-downs she had always worn. By now she was growing into a beautiful young lady and caught the eye of James E. Vandervort. He had been a Christian about two years when a friend invited him to Bradford Alliance Church to hear their new pastor. Vandervort had been troubled by some of the doctrinal teaching he had heard and the inconsistencies of those who taught it. He was thrilled by the preaching he heard in the Alliance church. "I listened closely to the preaching. He [Preacher] loved to preach the word, proclaim the transforming power of the Gospel, and exalt Jesus Christ as the one trustworthy Lord of the Christian lifestyle." Although he didn't know it right then, Preacher was modeling Vandervort's future ministry as he preached, prayed, teased children and played sports with the young people.

It wasn't long before Vandervort and Barbara started dating. He also started feeling the still small voice of the Lord calling him into the ministry. He was not alone among the young men in that small church. During Preacher's two-and-a-half years in Bradford, four of them were called to serve God. Preacher believed part of why God sent him to Bradford was to help prepare those four for the call to the ministry.

Jim and Barbara were soon engaged. One incident occurred during that time that would be talked about for years. Preacher, Freda and the boys had gone to bed and Barbara and Jim were in the living room discussing how badly they wanted to see Jim's parents come to know the Lord. They talked about ways they could impact his parents' lives through their influence, and then decided the best thing they could do at that very moment was pray about it. Before they had finished, Preacher called down to remind Barbara it was curfew time. They were so deep in prayer that they didn't hear Preacher. A while later and knowing Jim had still not left, he hurriedly got out of bed to go down and do "the lecture routine." Preacher's mind was so preoccupied with what he was going to say that he failed to pay attention to where he was going and stubbed his toe on the end of the bed. "Dad came storming downstairs but stopped midway when he saw us praying," she remembered. "He meekly turned around and went back upstairs and got into bed without saying a word.

[65]

Mother laid there until she couldn't contain her curiosity any longer and said, 'Well?' Dad replied gruffly, 'They're praying.'" Many times after that, Barbara's brothers asked her if she was really praying when she heard Preacher coming down the steps or was it a flash of brilliance on her and Jim's part to get on their knees.

It was while at Bradford that the Freeland family got their first television set — an old black-and-white someone gave them. Back then, it wasn't exactly proper for a pastor in western Pennsylvania to own one. So putting an antenna on the roof was not an option. Preacher would sometimes sneak up the stairs to watch a western or two on that old set. But most of the time all he saw was "snow."

As Preacher watched his little church grow, he felt in his heart that it was time for the congregation to move to a bigger and better location. He found a Jewish synagogue for sale in the downtown area and even made some preliminary negotiations to buy it. However, when he presented the idea to the church body, they decided they were not ready to make such a move. Preacher knew moving to the synagogue was the right direction to go and was disappointed the members of his church hadn't caught his vision.

Meanwhile, Jim applied to Nyack College to study for the ministry and he and Barbara set a wedding date. They were married in the Bradford Alliance Church on Aug. 28, 1953, with Preacher performing the ceremony. After learning that married couples could not attend Nyack together the first year, Jim instead applied to St. Paul Bible College in Minnesota. Although sad to lose Barbara, it thrilled Preacher to know her and Jim would be involved in full-time ministry for the Lord.

Preacher never asked the district superintendent about possible church openings while he was in Bradford. But both he and Freda felt that God wanted them somewhere else. As Christmas time came and went, he knew it would be his last one there.

Chapter 16

Answers To Prayer In Clearfield, PA

"Is any one of you sick? He should call the elders of the church to pray over him and anoint him with oil in the name of the Lord, and the prayer offered in faith will make the sick person well; the Lord will raise him up." **James 5:15 (NIV)**

In February 1954 Preacher received a call from the district superintendent asking if he would be willing to candidate for the position of pastor of the Clearfield (PA) Alliance Church. After praying about it for a few days, he agreed. Arriving for the weekend services, he found a small white wooden church that only seated about 100 or so people. "I sure wasn't going to some mega-church. The Lord gave us souls that night. I met with the church board and they invited me to be their pastor. I prayed about it for a day or so and accepted." Packing up the family again, he moved to Clearfield on March 1.

Clearfield, the county seat, was a small town of about 6,000 with Kurtz Brothers (School supplies, equipment and furniture) being the main industry. As they moved into the small wooden parsonage next to the church, they found it to be in pretty bad shape, particularly the basement. The church, too, was also in need of repairs. Jim, who turned 14 a few days after they arrived, Earl who was 11 and six-year-old Bob were thrilled, however, to find they would be living right next door to the fairgrounds — a built in playground. Although the flies were awful when the fair was in town — so big they could carry the livestock off, it seemed — they would spend countless hours playing there.

As in Union City and Bradford, the Lord blessed with souls for His Kingdom. "I was in God's will in Clearfield — a well-rounded church. I was the only paid person. I even had to be the secretary." But Preacher had solid elders to help him and when people came to the altar, they were trained to lead them to the Lord. The church grew so fast early on that they had to put chairs in the aisles to accommodate everyone. It didn't take long for Preacher to realize the church just wasn't big enough for what God had planned.

Just as in his previous pastorates, Preacher made it a point to get to know his congregation on a personal level. He set up priorities in his visitation schedule, realizing that some members needed more of his attention than others. And he set aside a part of every day to study the scriptures. After the Lord gave him an idea or specific scripture, he would refer back to files he kept on sermons he had previously preached and go to every source he had to get more information. Preacher's sermons always included illustrations that applied to the real world in which his congregation lived. "Remember, sermons may be doors but illustrations are windows.

A good illustration can open up a clear picture — might even wake someone up." Occasionally, even though he had spent hours preparing a particular sermon, Saturday would come without the satisfaction of knowing it was what God wanted him to preach. "Talk about sweating. Then you wake up about one-thirty in the morning and bang, there's the outline. Get up and write it down and go back and sleep like a baby." Preacher recognized that to be an affective pastor he had to allow the Holly Spirit to minister through him. As a result, his sermons were well-prepared and presented in such a way that everyone in the congregation was able to understand them. "One of the greatest compliments I ever had was from a little old lady who supposedly didn't have all of her buttons. She came up to me and said she understood every word I said. I gave her a hug and walked a long time with a bounce to my step."

By the time they had been in Clearfield for a year or so, it had become evident that both Jim and Earl were going to be very good athletes. During the five years they were there, they progressed from playing in youth leagues to junior high football, basketball and baseball, and finally all three sports in high school. Jim took great pride in the fact that, although his dad was busy with the church, he always made time to come see he and Earl play. "I remember my dad almost never missed a game and was there for many practices, too. I could always look in the stands and he was there. I know there were many times he had to make sacrifices and adjust his schedule... but he was always there." The high school football field was located at the fairgrounds next door to the parsonage, making it easy for Preacher to "sneak" over to practice during a break from studying for his Sunday messages. Both Jim and Earl played halfback in high school. Jim was good but Earl was faster, scoring five touchdowns in one game. When Jim graduated, he received a scholarship to the Valley Forge Military Academy as both a halfback and punter.

When the Freeland boys were not playing organized sports, they were busy doing other activities. And Preacher was never far away, always finding time to be there with his boys. Of course, what Jim and Earl (and later Bob) enjoyed most was hunting. On a bitter cold morning in December 1955, Preacher took Jim and Earl deer hunting. Jim was 15 and Earl had just turned 13, and both were armed with their 410 shotguns. They had not been in the field long when Jim spotted a big buck. "I shot the biggest seven point buck I had ever seen with the 410 shotgun my parents had bought for me for my twelfth birthday. I was so proud of that deer. We skinned it and laid it on the back porch. The next day it was missing. Dad said the garbage man must have mistakenly taken it. I was sick because I wanted those horns. Three months later I walked into the house after school and there was the buck, hanging in the place where my dad's deer had always hung. Mom and dad had gotten it mounted for me. What a surprise. They were going to see how long it would take for me to realize it was my buck hanging there — about thirty seconds. I still have that buck and it looks as good as ever. After all these years I still have never seen a bigger buck in the woods."

During his pastorate at Clearfield, Preacher was given an old trailer at the Alliance denomination-owned Mahaffey Camp not far away. There were always tremendous meetings at Mahaffey and he loved spending time there. The camp, located in ground hog territory, was so serene that A. W. Tozer, legendary Alliance preacher and author, once said there was nothing there but God and trees. While at the camp in the summer of 1956, Preacher decided to paint the trailer. He was standing on a folding chair with a quart of paint in his hand when the chair collapsed, sending paint everywhere including up his nose. Although he was only eight years old at the time, Bob never forgot that sight. "The three of us boys could not stop laughing as the paint rolled out of his nose and he was spitting paint out of his mouth. Dad, half mad and half laughing, could only say, 'Go ahead and laugh. I would laugh if I were you, too.' From that day on that has been the standard statement we all make anytime something happens like this to one of us."

While at the camp a few days later, Preacher stepped on a board with a nail in it. The next day, limping through the hospital while making sick calls back in Clearfield, a nurse friend asked him what the problem was. Learning he had stepped on a nail, she arranged for Preacher to get a tetanus shot. About three days later he and the family traveled to Canada where Preacher was to lead a camp meeting. The family arrived a couple of days early so the boys could spend time swimming in the lake. The Saturday the meeting was to start, Freda noticed a spot on Preacher's arm that was spreading. Thinking it was nothing, he preached that night and then went to bed.

About two in the morning, Preacher was hurting so bad he could barely turn over in bed. Every nerve in his body felt like it was on fire. Thinking he might have pinched a nerve, he got out of bed and walked around trying not to disturb Freda. Before long he was groaning like a bear and the whole cabin was awake. Freda ran an iron across his back, hoping it would ease the pain. When it got worse, Preacher dressed and went to the camp office to get an aspirin. Seeing his arm, they told him he needed to go to Puget Sound immediately and find a doctor. As Preacher drove the 10 miles or so down the dirt road to town, he hurt so badly he could hardly hold on to the steering wheel.

Preacher arrived in Puget Sound about six in the morning, and the only place he found open was a bar. Not knowing what else to do, he went inside — the first time he had been somewhere like that since he had been saved. "Some drunk sitting at the bar came over and said he knew a Doctor Dailey and had his phone number. That's how the Lord works sometimes. This guy was drunk, probably from the night before, but the Lord used him. I called the doctor and told him who I was and that I had to preach that morning. He said he was about ten minutes away from his office, which was just across the street from the bar, and he would meet me there."

Doctor Dailey examined Preacher and after finding out about the nail in his foot, asked him if he was taking any medication. Preacher assured him he was not, but did mention the tetanus shot. The doctor called Clearfield to find out more and then drove Preacher directly to the local hospital. By the time they arrived Preacher was paralyzed and could hardly breathe. As he remembered it, the only thing he could move was his eyeballs and those even hurt. Freda was summoned from the campground and told that Preacher was in bad shape and might not make it. From the time he arrived at the hospital until eleven that morning, the doctor and several nurses took turns checking on him, but with no improvement.

Back at the campground, the eleven o'clock service started and the entire congregation started praying for Preacher's healing. "All of a sudden from the top of my head to the toes of my feet a feeling went through me and I had no pain at all. It was just like you pulled a blanket off me. At about that time the doctor came in. I was moving my arms and he took his stethoscope out and checked me. I can see him just like it was yesterday. He leaned against the wall and asked me what I thought happened. Wow, how wide open can God open the door? I told him God had healed me. Freda came in and the three of us talked. I witnessed to him for an hour or so. His mother was a Christian and he knew a little bit of what I was talking about. I don't know if he came to know the Lord later, but I do know we had our own camp meeting in that hospital room."

Before he left the hospital, Dr. Dailey instructed him not to try to preach again for at least six months. Preacher followed that order — for one day. By Tuesday night he was back delivering the sermon God had showed him and he preached the rest of the camp meeting.

By now, Barbara and Jim had finished their first year at St. Paul and had enrolled at Nyack. Preacher received a letter from her with tear stains all over it. In it she told her dad she had been diagnosed with cancer and told she had less than a year to live. A specialist at a cancer clinic in New York had confirmed the prognosis. That was around April and his church in Clearfield along with the people at the Mahaffey Camp started praying for her and kept on the entire summer. For his part, Preacher never blinked. In fact, to an outsider, he didn't even seem overly concerned. His youngest son, Bob, learned from Preacher what the power and assurance of God really meant. "I will never forget the day dad found out that my sister Barbara had cancer and was given a few months to live. After he prayed about it a sense of peace came over him and he said, 'Don't worry, God is going to heal Barb.' God had told him in no uncertain words that He was going to take care of it. And that was all he needed to have perfect peace of mind. That peace was evident to me even as an eight-year-old boy." In late August or early September, Barb called to let the family know she had returned to the clinic and they could find no trace of cancer.

There was never a dull moment in the Freeland household. Jim and Earl spent countless hours riding their new three-speed black bicycles which Preacher had purchased at great sacrifice. On the evenings they were home and not at the ball field, they could be found playing ping-pong in the basement or shooting BB guns. As he got older, Bob would join them. All the boys were good shots and Jim felt like the times they spent in the basement were priceless. "I remember shooting literally thousands of BBs at a jar lid hanging on a string. Then going around and picking them up and shooting them again." They made a game of shooting the swinging lid, retaining shooter's privilege until someone missed.

Bob turned eight in January 1956 and did his best to pay careful attention to his dad's Sunday sermons. One he still remembers was entitled "Don't Miss the Boat." After the message, he accepted Christ. Preacher had seen all four of his children come to know the Lord. The days in Clearfield were, indeed, happy ones and the Freeland band — Jim on trumpet, Earl on trombone and Preacher on saxophone — continued their nightly in-home concerts. Preacher knew how to play one song on the piano and whenever he sat down on the stool, Jim knew exactly what he was going to sing:

> My mother-in-law she is dead — um ti di dee dee dee.
> She got caught in a folding bed — um ti di dee dee dee.
> Ever since my mother-in-law's been dead,
> Folks all want to buy that folding bed.
> For they all have mother-in-laws you see — um ti di dee dee dee.

But one problem still existed. The Alliance church had nowhere left to put people. They had tried unsuccessfully to purchase property to build on. Also, the church had developed such a wonderful reputation in the community they didn't want to move anyhow. The solution was brilliant in its simplicity. The congregation decided to build a new church "around" the existing one. The project made the front page of the local newspaper and they hardly missed a service. The rallying point for funds to build the church was two-dollar-a-week pledges. And just about everyone signed up. They also sold $200 bonds. The main industry in town then — and still is today — was Kurtz Brothers, and the superintendent there, Mr. Grile, was a member of the church. Seeing the need, he put his entire savings of $5,000 into the bonds. Many others took enormous steps of faith and the necessary funds came in.

In all, church members put in an estimated 1,100 hours of volunteer work to complete the project. For many it was a labor of love. Including Preacher. "I handled every brick that went into that crazy place. We actually tore the old church down and threw it out the windows of the new church." Tiling the basement was the last job left, and with just two days left before it was to be dedicated, Preacher worked through the night until blood ran out of his fingers. They had strung lights up so they could see to work after dark. Preacher remembered the inspector arriving about 10 p.m. the night before dedication and looking around. Preacher and several men had just finished pouring the final concrete and were dead tired. "All he [the inspector] wanted to do was complain about the lights. I had just about had it with that guy. That's the closest I ever came to giving a guy a sanctified punch. I could have decked him and not felt bad about it, but the Lord restrained me."

One incident that occurred during construction bears telling. Norman Kinnard was helping Preacher lay flooring when "someone" came up behind him and nailed his pants to the floor. Kinnard didn't even notice until he tried several times to scoot across the floor. The culprit, aka "June Bug" Freeland, was never discovered.

God poured out his blessings even more after the church was completed. At prayer meeting one night, a man named Joe Owens walked in off the street and asked if the church would pray for his sick baby. God healed the child and Owens became a regular attendee. Over the next few months, 16 members of his family came to know the Lord. Through Owens, Preacher met his brother Dick, who was still not a Christian. One day, snow on the ground, the two decided to go hunting in the mountains. "On the side of a mountain, I started talking to him about the Lord. We sat down on an old stump and I took out a New Testament. Just happened to have one in my pocket. We knelt down in the snow right there and he accepted the Lord."

Preacher's son, Earl, and Dick's son became close friends and Earl often visited in his home. One day Mr. Owen told Earl how his dad, Preacher, had led him to the Lord. The conversation turned to hunting, and Earl said something like if winning souls for Christ was his dad's favorite passion, killing bucks was certainly a close second. Dick Evans then mentioned he owned a piece of property on a mountain about 20 miles from Clearfield. He had drilled a well on the property with the intention of putting a trailer on it. Instead, he wondered if Preacher would like the property to build a hunting lodge, instead. The property was deeded to Preacher but it would be several decades, 1979 to be exact, before the Freelands finally got it built. From that time on, the week after Thanksgiving was set aside for Preacher and his three sons to meet at "Camp Horney" to hunt and swap yarns. The name, by the way, referred to all the deer horns they mounted on the wall. Preacher's son-in-law, by now Rev. James Vandervort, joined them on a couple of occasions. Bob recounted one of those times. "This hunter came by and asked who the guy was at the deer stand down the road. When I told him it was Reverend Jim Vandervort, my brother-in-law, he laughed and said he doubted if he would ever get a deer. He said that when he went by the guy was snoring so loud it would take a huge deer to wake him up." The family sold the property in 1998 when it became obvious Preacher would not be able to keep up with the walking required to enjoy the week.

But back to Clearfield. In early 1958 Preacher bought a new Oldsmobile Super 88. He had always wanted a bigger, heavier automobile and with its gray and white paint job and red pinstripes, it was the car he had always dreamed of. Jim was in his senior year of high school and had excelled academically and athletically. He was also admired by his peers for the stand he had taken for the Lord. On graduation night, instead of going to parties like most kids were doing, Jim and his girlfriend, who he would later marry, and another couple decided to go out to a nice restaurant about two hours away. Although Preacher and Freda were apprehensive about how late they would be out, they agreed to let Jim borrow the Olds. On the way back from the restaurant everyone in the car fell asleep, including Jim. He hit a bridge abutment and totally demolished Preacher's car. Thankfully, the Lord spared all four of them. "I remember calling mom and dad from the Tyrone hospital, expecting to be in big trouble. I'll never forget their response. They simply asked if everyone was all right. They told me not to worry, they could always get another car but never get another son like me. How many kids are lucky enough to have parents like that?" The accident was never mentioned again.

As 1958 swept by, Preacher realized his family was growing up. Barbara was married and away from home and Jim was attending Valley Forge Military Academy. The church was prospering and he knew that before long they would need to build again. That wouldn't be a problem, since by now, there were at least three millionaires who were regular members. In fact, the church at the point was giving over $100,000 a year to foreign missions alone. And although he loved the Clearfield Alliance Church with all his heart, Preacher had the feeling it wouldn't be his last pastorate.

As if to confirm this feeling, Preacher was asked to candidate at two churches in New York. After praying about it, he knew it was not God's will so he turned down both invitations. Another church in Texas also called, and again, after prayer, he declined. He knew it was not what God had planned for him and he didn't want to use their money to fly there for a free weekend vacation. Then, about a week or so after turning down the invitation from Texas, the phone rang again... who could it be now?

Chapter 17

Where In The World Is Portsmouth, VA?

"Taking the five loaves and the two fish and looking up to heaven, He gave thanks and broke the loaves. Then He gave them to His disciples to set before the people. He also divided the two fish among them all. They ate and were satisfied, and the disciples picked up twelve basketfuls of broken pieces of bread and fish. The number of men who had eaten was five thousand." **Mark 6:41-44 (NIV)**

The phone call was from Rev. Mason, superintendent for the Alliance's Virginia District, wanting to discuss an opening in Portsmouth, VA. They talked about the church in general terms for a few minutes, including the fact that they had already rejected three candidates. "We talked a little while and boy all of a sudden the Lord spoke to my heart and told me He wanted me to go down there and build a church." Although he loved Clearfield and knew absolutely nothing about Portsmouth, Preacher knew the Holy Spirit had spoken to him in no uncertain terms. "I told Freda after I hung up the phone to start packing, we were going to Portsmouth, Virginia. I didn't even know if the church would want me, only that the Lord had spoken to me and me to go there and build a church."

The Alliance Church in Portsmouth had been formed about 17 years before Preacher got the call to candidate. During the beginning years of World War II, Rev. Roy Forward, pastor of an Alliance church in neighboring Norfolk, felt burdened to start a church just across the Elizabeth River. God brought him in contact with the Charles Caswell family and a Sunday School program was pioneered in a housing project. It quickly grew and soon between 75 and 115 people were attending, many of them children and young adults. An evening Sunday vespers service was then added using local fundamental pastors. It wasn't long before the attendees began clamoring for a "real" church, feeling the recreation hall they were meeting in did not provide the right atmosphere.

With the Lord's leading, Rev. Forward and his newly-formed congregation began looking at rental properties. When they couldn't find the right building, they started seeking property to buy but found most available lots to be way too expensive. Then, in one of the many miracles God provided, property was secured in the Prentis Park section of the city. Since most if not all building materials were frozen due to the war effort, the church had to seek the Lord's help and guidance. In prayer, they were led to the scripture where Jesus fed the five thousand and the Holy Spirit made it abundantly clear if they would give what they had He would multiply it to feed the spiritually hungry. With the promises of God ringing in their ears and using whatever material they could get their hands on, the people began building the church with the first spade of dirt turned by Rev. Forward on February 22,

1942. Shortly after, Rev. Forward was appointed as missionary to Ecuador, South America, but not before laying the groundwork for what would become one of Portsmouth's most influential and successful churches.

The first full-time pastor of the Portsmouth Alliance Church was Harry Hardwick, a young man fresh out of Nyack College. He arrived during the early stages of construction and held the first service in the new church on September 22, 1942. Under his six-year ministry in Portsmouth, the church grew and an annex was added using bricks given to them from wartime buildings being demolished. One of the highlights of those early days was a 30-minute radio program that introduced folks, many for the first time, to the Portsmouth Alliance Church.

Reverend Hardwick felt the Lord calling him to other fields of labor and on December 1, 1948, Rev. James Strickland became the church's second pastor, a position he would hold until late September 1951. Portsmouth Alliance was without a pastor for the next few months, but used that time to build a new parsonage on property adjacent to the church. It was completed just in time for the April 13, 1952, arrival of Rev. Andrew Berkner and his family from White Plains, NY.

Under Rev. Berkner's steady hand, the church continued to grow requiring that a second annex be built. Toward the end of his stay, it became clear that even more church space was needed although there was no more room to build on the existing property. The church's executive board looked at new sites, but nothing developed. Reverend Berkner left in February 1959 to lead a church in Memphis, TN, and once again Portsmouth Alliance began praying for God to send His chosen one to lead them.

Reverend Earl Freeland was to be that man.

It was a beautiful spring day when Preacher received the call requesting he candidate for the church in Portsmouth. After telling Freda she might want to start thinking about packing up for another move, he spent the day reflecting on his ministry in Clearfield and how happy he and the family were there. His oldest son, Jim, had a good job, was engaged to be married, and had decided to make Clearfield his permanent home. Barbara and his son-in-law, Jim, were now attending Nyack College not too far away. Earl was following his older brother's footsteps as an outstanding athlete at Clearfield High School and little Bob was already showing a lot of promise, too. Preacher wondered why in the world he would want to leave. But he also knew that since the night he accepted the Lord, his only desire had been to be in His will. As he prayed that night before going to bed, he once again asked that God's will be done, even if it meant moving to Virginia. He also remembered telling himself, "I sure do hope they have deer in Portsmouth."

A few weeks later he drove alone the 400 or so miles to Portsmouth to preach the Sunday morning and evening services. His hosts for the weekend were Roy and

Delores Taylor, leaders in the church. After showing him around the city, the Taylor's took Preacher to their home in Elizabeth Manor. It was a Saturday evening and the first thing Preacher did after plopping down in an easy chair was kick off his shoes. Asked if he needed anything, he told them he would sure like to watch *Gunsmoke*. Preacher loved the banter between Marshall Matt Dillon and his deputy Chester Proudfoot. Roy and Delores were thrilled. Both had wondered if they could turn the television on while he was there.

Donald Smith, who would many years later serve as secretary of the governing board at Portsmouth Alliance, was a child of eight the Sunday morning Preacher candidated. "There was a curtain over the doorway that led from children's church into a long hallway that connected to the older part of the church. Reverend Freeland came by and stuck his head through the curtain — only his head and nothing else. Of course, this got all of our attention. Reverend Freeland asked us if we could sing. We wanted to show him how loud. I believe we sang *"Do Lord, Oh Do Lord, Oh Do Remember Me,"* our favorite song. All of us sang it for him at the top of our lungs. He was pleased."

The church hosted a get-together for Preacher after the morning service. After hearing him preach and seeing how well he related to people, and especially the children, they extended an invitation for him to become their pastor. Already knowing it was what the Lord wanted, he accepted. Preacher resigned his position in Clearfield effective June 1, 1959, and he, Freda, Earl and Bob headed for Portsmouth. Still another chapter in his life was about to begin... only this one would last him a lifetime.

Chapter 18

Bustin' At The Seams

"But in your hearts set apart Christ as Lord. Always be prepared to give an answer to everyone who asks you to give the reason for the hope that you have but do this with gentleness and respect." **1 Peter 3:15 (NIV)**

The Freeland family arrived in Portsmouth in early June and were shown around by the Knox's, a family who lived near the church and who had actually donated the land where it and the parsonage now stood. Their first impression of Portsmouth and the community named Prentis Park was very favorable and they could hardly wait to start their ministry there. As worshippers gathered Sunday morning, June 14,1959, they found a short greeting from their new pastor in the church bulletin:

— — —

Dear Friends,

We have been looking forward to this day for several weeks. It is good to be here and we are really looking forward to rich blessings from the Lord. Let us pray earnestly together for a great ingathering of souls.

In Him, Rev. Earl Freeland

— — —

Preacher was scanning the bulletin before preaching his first sermon and noticed a reminder that the church had developed a new system for designating gifts and tithes. In addition to earmarking money for current expenses, the pastor and missionary work, he was thrilled to see a category for building funds.

Pauline Beale and her husband, Bud, were among those in attendance that first Sunday. Like everyone else, she wondered what kind of pastor the Lord had sent them. Preacher's sermon was entitled "What is the Gospel According to You" and he related how most folks were familiar with the Gospels according the Matthew, Mark, Luke and John. But then he asked the congregation what were people seeing in their own lives. He ended with a very simple question: "What was the Gospel according to you?" Pauline recalled the first sermon years later and remembered what a profound impression it made on her. The hundred or so other people that Sunday morning left equally as challenged and certain that God had sent Preacher to be their shepherd and friend.

Preacher's first week in Portsmouth was a busy one. The day after delivering his first sermon marked the beginning of Vacation Bible School. It was the perfect opportunity for him to get to know some of the church people, and particularly the kids, on a personal level. And boy did he take advantage of it. The children loved how he would mess around and joke with them, and their parents would just stand back and grin. That Wednesday night, while the children were in their own classes, Preacher took the pulpit for the evening prayer meeting. As he looked out over the congregation, he saw a myriad of faces — business men and women, blue-collar workers, service personnel — people who had taken time out of their busy weeks to come into God's house. He sensed many were having a hard week and going through difficult times. That night Preacher spoke on the subject "Where I Lay My Burdens Down and He Lifts Me Up." This was the first of many, many times during his ministry in Portsmouth he would invite the congregation to turn their problems over to Him who cares and understands.

The week ended on Saturday night with Preacher learning first hand of one of the church's outreach ministries. As it did often, Alliance hosted a Portsmouth Youth for Christ meeting and Preacher sat back and smiled as he listened to young people from many area churches share their joy for Jesus.

The district superintendent, Rev. Dittmer, was present at the following Wednesday night prayer service and Preacher was officially installed as pastor. Little did anyone know the tremendous impact Preacher would have on the church and just importantly, the Portsmouth community, in the ensuing years. From the beginning, the church was filled with people anxious to hear the Gospel. Souls started being saved and it wasn't many weeks before they started putting chairs in the aisles to accommodate the congregation. That first summer, it seemed like the music from the crowded church on Des Moines Avenue could be heard throughout the entire city. The church's reputation for having a great music program was only strengthened after Preacher arrived. Pauline Beale's husband, Bud, jokingly remarked many times over the years that Rev. Freeland was the only pastor he knew who could sing almost every hymn in the book and then preach for 30 minutes.

Those first few months were something of a culture shock for the Freelands — especially when it came to Southern food. One day Mrs. Knox dropped by and asked Freda if her family like salad. Freda said of course so, thinking she meant a tossed salad with dressing. The next day Mrs. Knox brought over a large bag of salad greens fresh from her garden and left them on Preacher's back porch. When Preacher and Freda found the bag, they couldn't figure out why someone one had left dirty leaves so they threw them in the trash. Butter beans were another vegetable they had to get used to, since they were served at just about every meal they enjoyed with members of the church.

With the summer coming to a close, Preacher realized it was time to think about enrolling Earl and Bob in school. Earl would be a sophomore and they lived in the part of Portsmouth served by Woodrow Wilson High School. However, one day Preacher and the boys happened to ride by Cradock High School and noticed the football team working out. They stopped to watch practice and afterwards Preacher introduced himself to the coach, Larry Weldon. "We talked and he asked me about the boys. I just happened to mention that Earl had scored five touchdowns in one game for Clearfield High School in Pennsylvania." Coach Weldon pulled a few strings and, not surprisingly, both boys were enrolled in schools in Cradock that fall. Earl became a starting linebacker and halfback for Cradock High that season, and Preacher was asked to be the team chaplain.

Although certain he was in the will of God, there were times during those first few months when Preacher couldn't help thinking about the church and people he had left behind in Clearfield. His oldest boy, Jim, was doing great there at Kurtz Brothers and he was engaged to be married to his fiancé Judy Eckly. So in August, Preacher loaded the car with Freda, Earl and Bob and headed back to Pennsylvania to conduct the marriage ceremony of Jim and Judy. Preacher thoroughly enjoyed the short time he spent with his old friends and church members in Clearfield, but the whole family agreed they were glad to be "home" when they arrived back in Portsmouth.

The first year in Portsmouth flew by for Preacher. The entire congregation became part of his family and they spent many evenings and Saturdays fellowshipping together. Sometimes it would be fishing, bowling or miniature golf. Other times it would just be going to a restaurant for pie and coffee. Virginia Cuthriell, one of the matriarchs at Portsmouth Alliance, reminisced about the early months of Preacher's ministry. "He had his humorous side and was quite a joke cracker. On fishing trips he was known to put live fish in his companions' hip pockets. Often a group from the church would go to Yings, a favorite local Chinese restaurant. Preacher was always the recipient of an ugly rubber chicken with head and feet served to him by Mrs. Ying in a covered dish. He enjoyed the joke as much as we did. He loved children and many Sundays he greeted the church folks with little people wrapped around his legs."

One Saturday afternoon early on Preacher joined the church softball team for an afternoon game. After popping up and grounding out the first few times, he finally got a hit and, while rounding first base, tripped and seriously injured his knee. After surgery and a few days recuperating and driving Freda and the boys crazy, he returned to the pulpit and preached from a wheelchair. Although his days playing for the church team were limited after that, he could always be found leaning over the fence watching the game — Alliance jacket and hat proudly worn. My son, Bud, Jr., remembers it well. "I started playing for Alliance in the mid-1980s. We were a real powerhouse and had two men's teams and two women's teams. There were some nights when all four of our teams would be playing at the same time at different fields all across the city. We'd get to church on Sunday and one of the players would say they saw Preacher Freeland at the game. Then another player from one of our other teams would say, 'No you didn't he was at our game.' And then one of the players on the women's team would chime in, 'You're both wrong, Preacher was at our game.' I really do believe he was at all three or four games some nights and at the same time. Now that was a miracle." Over the years, much of Preacher's witnessing was in some way connected to his love for sports.

As preacher began his second year of ministry in Portsmouth, the need for a larger place to worship began taking on a sense of urgency. The church was literally bursting at the seams. Cautiously at first, the search for suitable land to build a new church began. Virginia Cuthriell was one of many who could sense the Lord working in their midst. And Rev. Freeland was a big part of that reason. "He was love personified. He ate with us, he cried with us, he lived among us and became one of us. Through highs and lows, through laughter and tears, through crisis and crownings he was there. There were times when he spent most of a night sharing with families in their sorrows, vigils by hospital beds until the last breath was drawn — then continue his ministering to the families until the dawn brought renewal."

Donald Smith was one of those who witnessed first-hand Preacher and Freda's Christian love and hospitality. In August 1960, his mother, Doris, had open heart surgery at the University of Virginia. She was one of the first people in the eastern United States to have such an operation using a revolutionary new machine that kept the heart pumping while surgeons worked directly on the problem. The operation and recovery time lasted many weeks, and Donald's father and grandparents had taken all their vacation time to be with her. That meant Donald and his sister, Joy, would have no one to look after them. No problem. "Families of the church took turns adopting us. When school started in September it was the Freeland's turn and we stayed with them until October. The Bible says the world will know us by our love. Reverend and Mrs. Freeland and the church family showed their love to us in a wonderful way."

Chapter 19

The Game Of Eternal Life

"But we had to celebrate and be glad, because this brother of yours was dead and is alive again; he was lost and is found." **Luke 15:32 (NIV)**

As the Portsmouth Alliance Church in Prentis Park continued to grow, Preacher found there were often not enough hours in the day to accomplish all he wanted to do. But he still found time for Earl and Bob. As mentioned, the fall of 1959 found both boys in schools in Cradock. Earl, though new to the area and small in statue, quickly earned the reputation of being one of the toughest linebackers the school had ever had. He also was an outstanding halfback and rarely if ever came off the field. But the true MVP — Most Valuable Preacher — was his dad. Preacher served as Cradock's team chaplain all the way through the 1966 season when his youngest, son, Bob graduated from there. And what an impression he made on those athletes.

Ralph Gaebhart, now an elder in the Portsmouth Alliance Church, was an all-city quarterback at Cradock High School and remembers meeting Pastor for the first time. "I began my first year on the varsity football team at Cradock in 1961. Just before the first game, Rev. Earl Freeland was introduced to the team as our chaplain and led us in prayer. That was the first time I remember seeing Rev. Freeland even though he probably had visited some of our summer practices. Like most others who met him, I noticed his warmth, his smile and his caring manner. As he led us in prayer, he confirmed all of those impressions. He prayed for safety and sportsmanship but not for winning the game. I was familiar with the Freeland name, since I watched the Craddock football team for years and knew about that good linebacker named Earl Freeland."

Late that season, Coach Weldon announced that the team would be attending a Sunday night service at Portsmouth Alliance Church. Gaebhart remembered thinking it was odd that Rev. Freeland and Coach Weldon were friends since he used a lot of profanity and did not appear to be a Christian. It was a fair assessment. Weldon, who had served as a backup quarterback to the legendary Sammy Baugh with the Washington Redskins for two years, had attended Presbyterian College in Clinton, SC. And while he knew about spiritual matters, he did not practice them in his life. On that Sunday night, the entire team — all wearing neckties — sat as a group in front of the church and was introduced to the congregation. Gaebhart remembers feeling a little uneasy. "I had attended Highland Baptist Church all my life. It was a Southern Baptist church with good Bible-based preaching. So entering the Alliance church that night seemed a little strange. The feeling quickly disappeared as we sang a couple of hymns that were the same ones I would have been singing that night at my church. Reverend Freeland delivered an evangelical sermon from God's Word. The love and joy that characterized Reverend Freeland was communicated as he challenged the congregation and the team. I remember thinking that he was preaching the same truths that I had been taught in my church."

Preacher continued the practice each year of inviting the Cradock High School football team to an evening service. And like he always did, he would invite the unsaved to make a decision for Christ. None of the players ever responded to the invitation... that is, until the 1964 season. Preacher and Freda fixed hot dogs and lemonade for the team in their yard before the service and then he preached that night on the prodigal son. He entitled his sermon "What Shall I Do With Jesus" and chose as his text four verses from the Gospel of Matthew:

"Every tree that bringeth not forth good fruit is hewn down, and cast into the fire. Wherefore by their fruits ye shall know them. Not every one that saith unto me, Lord, Lord, shall enter into the kingdom of heaven; but he that doeth the will of my Father which is in heaven. May will say to me in that day, Lord, Lord, have we not prophesied in thy name? And in thy name have cast out devils? And in thy name done many wonderful works? And then will I profess unto them, I never knew you; depart from me, ye that work iniquity." **Matthew 8:19-23 (NIV)**

As Preacher began his message, he repeated the title, "What shall I do with Jesus, which is called the Christ?" He then poured out his heart to a full congregation, including the Cradock football team and their coach. "This question has been asked to every nation and every individual since time began. Like the crowd before Pilot that fateful day, most nations have cried out 'crucify Him.' They have become nations of blood — pugnacious, scornful, selfish, uncooperative. Blood has been shed and heads have rolled under their reign. Their men have become machines. Life has become a living hell — home a place of sorrow, crime abounds, hatred is a rule and love is a forgotten note, never to be played on the melody of life."

Up to this point, the sermon had essentially been general in nature and covered the world as a whole. But Preacher was just warming up. Now he addressed his remarks to his congregation, and especially to the football team and their coach. Weldon could feel the heat rising under his white-starched dress shirt and probably thought someone in the church had turned up the furnace. Some of the players began to feel a little uncomfortable, too.

Try to listen back to Preacher's words:

— — —

Now the individual is asked, what will you do with Jesus? Little did Pilate imagine when he went to sleep on Thursday that Friday would be the greatest day of crisis in all of his life. Friday would be a red-letter day in his life from then on. Friday he made a decision that would not only affect his days on earth, but eternity as well. Pilate is called by the rulers to the Judgement Hall. I see him as they awaken him — grudgingly he puts on his judicial robes and stalks to the judicial throne.

From this throne he has sentenced many other men to death, yet when Jesus is brought before him, something begins to happen in his hardened heart. A conscience he though was dead is brought to life. Somehow he is aware of a strange sensation, like he was standing in the presence of God. I wonder if his past life did not flow before him, if his memory was filled with regret.

I believe there comes special moments in every man's life — moments of decision — when God sort of stops him in his tracks and puts the question to him. This was Pilot's moment. What would he do? Confess or conform? Christ or the crowd? The crowd cried conform — do away with Him; have nothing to do with Him; be like us; crucify Him; cast Him away; claim with us He is not the Son of God but merely a carpenter. As so many do, Pilate chose the crowd.

The cries of the crowd are still upon us. We live in a puppet world. Someone pulls a string and we follow. We feel like we have to conform in what we wear, where we go, what we drink and on and on. Men will not think for themselves. How about you? Crown or crucify? The Bible asks each of you the same question tonight. What will you do with Jesus? Some will curse him. Some will try to evade and ignore Him. Some will try to forget Him. But the question still must be answered. How will you answer?

— — —

Preacher then gave the altar call. In addition to Coach Weldon, 15 Cradock High School football players surrendered their lives to Christ that night.

A senior by then, Gaebhart still cherishes that night. "The players going forward in front of their peers showed the power of that moment. And Coach Weldon going forward was almost unbelievable. He was the toughest, most profane man I had ever been around. I think everyone was asking themselves if this man could really change, but he had made his commitment in front of forty teenagers who would be watching him every day. To the surprise of many, he was a changed man. He was still a tough football coach, but his emotions were under control. The profanity was gone from his vocabulary. My hope was that the change in Coach Weldon's life would make an impression on the team and others to follow."

Chapter 20

Lord, You Really Want Us To Build There?

"Therefore everyone who hears these words of mine and puts them into practice is like a wise man who built his house on the rock." **Matthew 7:24 (NIV)**

The church was buzzing with activity as Preacher prepared for his first Christmas message at Portsmouth Alliance in 1959. There were so many things that needed to be accomplished for the Lord, not the least of which was building a new place of worship. For his sermon Preacher selected as his scripture **James 1:17** and entitled it "What Do You Want For Christmas?"

"Every good and perfect gift is from above, coming down from the Father of the heavenly lights, who does not change like shifting shadows." **James 1:17 (NIV)**

Preacher recounted how good the Lord had been to the Alliance church family and reminded the congregation that is was only through His grace that good things came their way. He then admonished each person to reflect on God's goodness during the Christmas season and to seek His will in the coming year. Lastly, in the special way he had with children, he admitted he wouldn't mind receiving a chocolate bar or two and it was right for them to ask for a toy or two.

Preacher continued to serve as the only paid employee, sometimes getting as much as $60 a week in the love offering designated for his salary. He and the governing board investigated and just as quickly rejected several possible building sites for a new church, believing they had not found the spot God had already chosen for them. Preacher often reminded the governing board that God would let them know when and where to build.

As Easter approached, Preacher prayed that God would give him a message that would stir the hearts. Going through some old sermon notes, he came across one he had preached in the Bradford church on Easter Sunday 1953. God told him his new church family needed to hear that same message. On Easter Sunday morning 1960, Preacher turned to Romans and read his scripture:

"He who did not spare his own Son, but gave him up for us all — how will he not also, along with him, graciously give us all things." **Romans 8:32 (NIV)**

He then poured out his heart in a message entitled "Behind the Cross." In it, he stressed three main points: What the cross meant to God; what it meant to Jesus; and finally, what it means to me. As he painted a word picture of Jesus hanging on the cross, Preacher made it clear that Jesus died for the sins of every single man, women and child there that day.

As the days and weeks hurried by, Preacher found himself becoming more anxious about finding a building site for the new Portsmouth Alliance Church. Then he remembered scripture admonishing him not to be anxious about anything and that God was in control. Still, the church builder in him cried out for an answer to their need. Preacher was driving along Portsmouth Boulevard a few weeks later (early June 1960) when the Lord spoke to him. "I had been in Portsmouth about a year and was driving past where the church is now. We had investigated and decided against several places. I was alone, and the Lord told me to stop. I looked over and saw what looked like a small lake. I said, 'Lord, surely you don't mean there?'"

Although there was no "For Sale" sign on the property, Preacher noticed a small green house adjacent to it so he went up and knocked on the door. "A little old lady with humped shoulders came to the door. She was having a bad attack of asthma and having trouble catching her breath. I introduced myself and mentioned the property next door. She said she and her husband owned it and I would have to talk to him. I asked if it would be all right for me to come back that night and talk to her husband and she said sure. I had prayer with her and left. I went back that night and that old man, rough as a corn cob, said the land was tied up with a real estate agent until January. I said, 'Okay, we're just going to ask the Lord about it.' So I had prayer and left."

When he told some of the board members where he had been, they just laughed. That same exact piece of property had been looked at years before and remembered as being a landing field for seagulls. Virginia Cuthriell, who had attended Portsmouth Alliance since its inception, remembered it well. "Circa 1942-43. A young twenty-eight year old pastor stood on the grounds of 5809 Portsmouth Boulevard. At that time God made it quite clear that this would be the home of the Portsmouth Alliance Church. As he looked over the site, considering its immensity and all that would be involved — his youth, inexperience, family and no officially formed church — he felt that he was not the one build it. However, in his heart he knew some day this would happen. That young preacher was Harry T. Hardwick, first pastor of the Portsmouth Alliance Church."

Later that week, while preparing for the Sunday morning message, Preacher started thinking about that property on Portsmouth Boulevard. He also surveyed his early life and how he had served the devil with everything in him until Jesus stepped into his life. Finally, he remembered how God had told him he was going to Portsmouth to build a church. Tears welled in his eyes as he thought of wasted years. Then a simple Bible verse from Psalm 30 came to his mind, "*Joy comes in the morning.*"

Feeling like a new man, again, he got back to work. While praying, Preacher recalled a sermon he had preached a couple of times at his previous pastorates. He turned in his Bible and read:

> "Then Saul said, I have sinned. Come back, David my son. Because you considered my life precious today, I will not try to harm you again. Surely I have acted like a fool and have erred greatly." **I Samuel 26:21 (NIV)**

In checking his files, he discovered he had preached from that same verse in Bradford on December 9, 1951, and also in Clearfield in December 1955. He would revisit it again in a Sunday message in Portsmouth in 1978.

On this particular Sunday in June 1960 he used the verse to preach a sermon on "Men Who Play the Part of the Fool." The points he shared with his flock that day were: Satan made a fool of me; God made me a son; Satan robbed me of years of life; and, God has given me life — life eternal. As he checked the church and turned out the lights after the service, Preacher's thoughts again turned to that awful looking property on Portsmouth Boulevard. He remembered thinking, "If I just close my eyes I can see a beautiful church filled with people praising the Lord." He was sure God was going to give them that property.

The next week he returned to the little green house and borrowed a tractor from Mrs. Anderson. He told her he was curious as to what was under all that water and, after running the tractor over it, was surprised to find the ground fairly solid. He then had a friend take a topography survey of the site, who discovered the land was 11 inches low forming a basin which collected water. Preacher hadn't told the governing board he was going back, but when he reported his findings, they agreed to pray if this was the place the Lord wanted them to build His church. One board member, half kidding, suggested they also pray that God would kill the seagulls and dry up the land like He did at the Red Sea. Later, as they checked further into the property, they found it covered over 10 acres and was on the market for $35,000. Preacher and the church then started praying the land would remain unsold until the end of the year so they could deal directly with the Andersons. Although they didn't go to church or serve the Lord, Preacher continued to visit Mrs. Anderson on a regular basis and pray with her because of her sickness.

The rest of 1960 seemed to fly by. And so did Preacher's son, Earl, as his younger brother Bob remembered it. Since they lived outside their regular school district, Preacher had driven Earl to Cradock High School each day the previous year and then picked him up after school or practice. Now a senior, Earl had gotten his own car and Preacher missed those treasured moments he spent with him driving back and forth. According to Bob, it did allow Preacher more time for prayer. "Under the wheel of the car, Earl had a heavy foot and got several speeding tickets. I remember mom and dad in their room praying for him a lot."

One of the last sermons he preached that year came on Sunday morning during the Christmas season. Entitled "God's Unusual Gifts" and supported by **II**

Corinthians 9:15 which reads *"Thanks be to God for His indescribable gift."* Preacher spoke of God's gift of conscience to convict; His gift of capacity for a God that nurtures a desire to seek' and His gift of love as set forth in the Gospel of John:

"For God so loved the world that he gave his one and only Son, that whoever believes in him shall not perish but have eternal life." **John 3:16 (NIV)**

Chapter 21

Wow! A New Church

"I intend, therefore, to build a temple for the Name of the Lord my God, as the Lord to my father David when he said, Your son whom I will put on the throne in your place will build the temple for my name." **I Kings 5:5 (NIV)**

Preacher did his best to show the patience of Job as he waited for the new year to arrive. Not wanting to appear too eager, he waited an entire day before going to see the Andersons. On January 2, 1961, he knocked on the door of the little green house already knowing in his heart that the property had not been sold. Once confirmed, Preacher asked Mr. Anderson if he'd be interested in seeing a church built on his property next door. Anderson thought about it a minute and then told Preacher he'd rather have a church there than a filling station. Getting up his nerve, he next asked how much he wanted for the property. Then Preacher held is breath. "He looked over to his wife and said they had talked it over and would sell us the property for fifteen thousand dollars. And they didn't want any interest. Boy, I was ready to go through the ceiling — camp meeting right there!" Preacher remembered Mr. Anderson looking him square in the eye and telling him he was the only pastor who had ever come to the house and prayed with his wife. "That broke the gates. I told him me and the Lord would be back."

The church decided it would take about $85,000 to build the church, plus the money for the property. A quick look at what they had in the building fund showed they had a long, long way to go. They would need someone to give them a loan. Meanwhile, the church members started saving their extra money for a down payment on the lot. The excitement spilled over into children's Sunday School. Donald Smith remembered as a young boy seeing the underwater property the church wanted to buy. "It looked like a lake. We called it a landing place for ducks. I also remember in Sunday School we had a small replica of the new church and would put our offerings in it every Sunday. We were told ten cents would buy a brick so ever dime we contributed would buy a brick for the new church."

Preacher and the governing board spent most of January being turned down by every loan company in the area. The story was always the same. Because of the size of the church congregation, banks didn't believe they would be able to pay off the loan. Preacher would tell them the one thing he was certain of was that God wanted a church on the property and not a swimming hole for seagulls and ducks.

The search for someone to make them a loan dragged into February. Preacher and the governing board were so sure they were in God's will they put the church on Des Moines Avenue up for sale. But still nobody would lend them a penny. Sitting in his living room. Preacher again thought about his life and how God had worked one miracle after another in his ministry. There had been so many good times, just he and the Lord. Picking up his Bible, he turned to the Gospel of John and read the story of Jesus walking on the water:

"When evening came, his disciples went down to the lake, where they got into a boat and set off across the lake for Capernaum. By now it was dark, and Jesus had not yet joined them. A strong wind was blowing and the waters grew rough. When they had rowed about three or four miles, they saw Jesus approaching the boat, walking on the water, and they were afraid. But he said to them, "It is I, don't be afraid." Then they were willing to take him into the boat, and immediately the boat reached the shore where they were heading." **John 6:16-21 (NIV)**

After he had finished and fearing he might be trying to do too much on his own, Preacher got down on his knees as he had done thousands of times before and invited Jesus to take complete control of his life. He then got up and started preparing his sermon for up the upcoming Sunday service.

That Sunday morning, Preacher read from that same sixth chapter of John and delivered a sermon entitled "Night and Jesus Was Not There." He painted a picture of the good times Jesus and his disciples had together walking by the sea. And all the times they had sat at His feet and witnessed the mighty acts of the matchless Son of God. He then switched gears and said, "Now the storm was howling, rain beating, waves rising, no stars, fear of the pitch black night. And Jesus was not there." Sitting on the edge of the pews, the congregation listened as Preacher invited them to look out into the midst of their own storm and see Jesus drawing nigh. Including himself, he reminded them Christians are so often absorbed rowing the boat themselves that they do not see Him standing there. As the service drew to a close, Preacher invited everyone to invite Jesus aboard their ship. After singing *"Turn Your Eyes Upon Jesus,"* everyone there flooded the altar to spend time talking with the One who calms our every sea.

The following week, while reading the evening newspaper, Preacher came across an article detailing how the American National Bank in Portsmouth had recently loaned a church $1 million dollars for a building project. The story also noted that Frank D. Lawrence, president of the bank, was a member there. Lawrence was one of the city's most successful businessmen and was also the owner of the Portsmouth Cubs, a professional baseball team in the Class B Piedmont League. Portsmouth Park, where his team played, was considered to be the finest privately-owned stadium in the country and he was regarded by many sports experts as the top-rated operator in Minor League baseball. As Preacher read the article, he remembered that the American National Bank was one of the many that had turned down his application for a loan.

Preacher called the bank and got an appointment to see Lawrence. With church résumé and newspaper article in hand, he met Lawrence the next day and, getting right to the point, asked him why the Portsmouth Alliance Church had been turned down for a loan. Lawrence laughed and said that was an easy one — Preacher's church didn't have enough people to guarantee the loan would be paid back. Preacher may not have been a math whiz back in high school, but he knew how to count and multiply his church flock. He started riddling Lawrence with questions about his own church. "I asked him how many he had in his church. We had one hundred and twenty-five on our roll, and he said his church had four hundred. I then asked him how many of them actually attended on Sunday morning and he said about two hundred. I said how about Sunday night and he said about fifty. I said how about Wednesday night and said maybe twenty-five. Well, I had my statistics with me. I told him, Mr. Lawrence, you have four hundred on your roll but only about fifty show up on Sunday night. We average more than a hundred on Sunday and Wednesday nights. I looked him straight in the eye and asked him if he would rather have four hundred people say they belonged to the American National Bank or have one hundred people come in and actually do business every day. He looked at me and said, 'You're talking about quality and not quantity.' I said you got it, had prayer with him and left."

A few days later, Lawrence called Preacher and told him he had gotten a loan for the church. But, and this was a big but, the church would have to come up with collateral. After meeting with Preacher earlier in the week, Lawrence had driven to Richmond, VA, to see if he could get a loan approved. When he was told it wouldn't be possible, it made him so mad he flew to New York and got an insurance company there to agree to lend Portsmouth Alliance the money. The board at his bank agreed as long as the church could provide the collateral.

Preacher went to see Mr. Anderson and told him the good news. His church had gotten the loan it needed to build the church. But there was one small problem. They didn't have anywhere near the amount needed for the collateral. Anderson solved the problem by signing the property over to Portsmouth Alliance Church so they could use it as a show of good faith to the bank. The church agreed to pay the Andersons $5,000 a year for three years, all of it interest free. With a big smile on his face, Preacher remembered what he told that man on the street in Nyack about his Father owning the cattle on a thousand hills. Only now, Preacher thought, He also owned the landing field for every seagull in Portsmouth.

After receiving the loan, the church started devising ways to make the monthly payments. They sold bonds and took two-dollars-a-week pledges. There was real excitement in the little church in Prentis Park. Donald Smith remembered a "march" offering one Sunday morning to raise funds to pay on the lot. "People had saved and collected money and row by row we marched up to the front of church and put it in the offering plate." Nearly $5,000 was raised that day, a third of what was needed to pay off the Andersons.

It seemed like some type of miracle, big or small, occurred just about every week. Enter Austin Peterson, a respected mechanical engineer who had been a member of the Union City Alliance Church in Pennsylvania a decade or so before when Preacher had been there. Somehow he got word that his former pastor was once again preparing to build a church. He showed up one day in Portsmouth and told Preacher he would be happy and honored to save the church some money. Peterson went back home and immediately drew plans for the new building down to the last detail. Christian friends are friends for a lifetime.

Armed with a loan, a blueprint and a property full of seagulls and other waterfowl, the church set Easter Sunday 1961 as groundbreaking for the Portsmouth Alliance Church on Portsmouth Boulevard. Now it was time to go to work. The first step was to haul in dirt to fill "Lake Freeland." Some folks, including Preacher, wondered if there was enough dirt in Portsmouth to get the job done. Preacher showed up to "supervise" every day, hands on hips and a big smile on his face. Roy Taylor, a leader in the church, was a building contractor and let the church use his name on the needed permits. He recommended a man named Paul Spruill to level the dirt. Preacher took an instant liking to him and started telling Spruill about Jesus. It wasn't many days later that Preacher led Spruill to the Lord. "Paul was a real worker. He would bring his tractor in and work and work, never charging us a dime." Preacher remembered showing up one day and not seeing a single seagull. He knew that must mean Spruill had finished the job.

Next on the list was laying the foundation. One of Taylor's employees, Lonnie Askew, was a hulk of a man who did concrete work. Although he had never laid a foundation before, he agreed to tackle the job. After all, he mentioned to Preacher, concrete is concrete. Askew was a fine Christian and before starting the project, he and Preacher got down on their knees in the corner of the lot and, in the mud, prayed. They confessed to the Lord neither knew the first thing about laying a foundation and would really appreciate His help and wisdom. Before pouring concrete, they first had to put in 116 pilings. With divine inspiration, they put steel rods in as well to provide stronger support and years later someone noted the church had never had a single crack. Preacher and Askew were on the worksite bright and early every morning and would work most of the day. Preacher would then stay up late at night studying and preparing for Sunday and Wednesday night services. Despite the hectic schedule, he never missed a single visitation. Arriving at the hospital an hour or so after leaving the property in his best Sunday suit, nurses would greet Preacher with a warm smile. Often, part of their grin was triggered by the mud on his shoes and on the cuffs of his suit.

Preacher also continued to make friends in the community. Two of these were Carl and Edna Rose. Their two twin boys, Danny and Donnie, were football teammates of Earl and through them Preacher met their parents. Donnie Rose was an all-state football player at Cradock and later starred for the University of South Carolina. Preacher would go to Carl Rose's butcher shop, buy a soda, and talk about the boys. He used that opportunity to tell Rose about the Lord and it wasn't long before his entire family started coming to Alliance regularly.

Living next door to Preacher was a young boy named Billy Knowles. The Bible often mentions how little children loved to be around Jesus. Knowles, as did countless other children, felt the same way about Preacher, who always had a tall tale to tell and a piece of candy to give. Knowles remembered often climbing the fence and running over to find Rev. Freeland. Knowles would later in life show that same love and concern for hundreds of young men as a highly successful high school baseball coach and then as athletic director at nearby Western Branch High School in Chesapeake.

As in most churches, there were always romances blossoming at Alliance. And once again, one of Preacher's own children was in love. Earl was dating a beautiful young lady in the church, Joyce Bridges, and it was obvious to everyone God had brought them together. As June arrived, Preacher found himself preparing to attend Earl's high school graduation and wedding at the same time. Earl graduated from Cradock on June 6, 1961, and was married four days later. Preacher and Freda found themselves with only one child left at home, their youngest son Bob.

That same month, a young man named Chuck Conti, who had a beautiful singing voice, accepted the Lord as his personal Savior. Raised Catholic, he had started attending the Portsmouth Alliance in 1955 while dating Barbara Neal. Agreeing to attend prayer meeting was the only way he was allowed to see her. When Preacher arrived during the summer of 1959, Conti found another reason to attend the church — to hear Preacher sing. He and Barbara became man and wife and he and Preacher became close friends. After accepting the Lord, Conti joined the choir. He would eventually become a featured soloist at Alliance and in 1969 Preacher turned over the duties of song leader to him — a position he would hold for many years. Although they talked about the services, Preacher left it up to Conti to choose the songs and choruses. Preacher called Conti, who worked at the local Ford plant, "the signing mechanic" and Conti often referred to Preacher as "Rabbi Freeland." Countless numbers of people were blessed by Conti's music ministry and today he is singing tenor in God's choir in Heaven.

The foundation for the new church was finished late that summer and the basic bed arms started going up. Almost every day, while working alongside the hired workers, Preacher would look up and see a church member who had stopped by to check on the progress. He would throw up his hand and without missing a beat continue to work. By the time September arrived, one wall was up and Preacher would "brag" to anyone who would listen how fast construction was going. The devil must have been listening. Word came that Hurricane Ethel was making a big fuss and headed straight for Portsmouth. Seemed like a good time for another miracle. "I had been going to McLean Building Supply for material and became friends with the foreman. I went to his office and he wanted to know what I was going to do about Ethel. He reckoned, a little tongue in cheek, that the hurricane might just blow our one wall down. Without thinking I told him we were going to pray and ask the Lord to turn the hurricane away from our building. He laughed and I left. Well, we started praying and that old hurricane turned out to sea."

Shortly after the second wall went up, another dangerous hurricane was predicted to hit Portsmouth. The church again prayed, and Preacher found himself once again in McLeans talking to the foreman. In a voice loud enough for all the guys to hear, the foreman greeted Rev. Freeland as "the preacher who prays hurricanes out to sea." And that's exactly what happened. Still, Preacher felt he could do just fine with no more hurricane scares that season. Perhaps thinking about the walls of Jericho falling in the Old Testament had a little something to do with it.

With only the four walls up, the church decided to have a Thanksgiving praise service on the site of the new church. Chairs were brought in and the site was filled with worshippers gathered to give thanks for His bountiful goodness. It was also a time of great rejoicing and anticipation. In was sometime during that weekend that Preacher remembered thanking the Lord for teaching him skills like welding back when he was living in sin.

As the holiday season quickly approached, it dawned on Preacher this would be last Christmas the Portsmouth Alliance Church would celebrate on Des Moines Avenue. After much prayer, he chose for his Sunday message a scripture he had used at the Clearfield Alliance in 1956:

> "When the angels had left them and gone into heaven, the shepherds said to one another, Let's go to Bethlehem and see this thing that has happened, which the Lord has to us about." **Luke 2:15 (NIV)**

On that bitterly cold morning, Preacher invited his church family to travel with him to the little town of Bethlehem. But first, he rejoiced in the progress they were making toward finishing construction of the new church and reminded them that in a few short months they would be making another journey — a journey to the new church and the beginning of a new chapter in the life of Portsmouth Alliance. After reading the scripture, Preacher then took everyone who was there that day on a joyous trip to Bethlehem — by prophecy; by remembrance; and by faith.

The first couple of months of 1962 were hectic to say the least. Preacher continued to work long hours at the building site while at the same time keeping up with his duties as a pastor. He worried he would get mixed up and either be setting tile in his "preaching suit" or visiting a church member in the hospital wearing dirty coveralls. Still, things were going well with the construction, although it did take a miracle or two to keep the project on track. Preacher remembered an instance when the building inspector, clipboard in hand, stopped by and said he needed to take a look at the choir loft. "That buzzard said we had to get another eight-inch steel beam and put it across the choir loft as support. I guess he had to find something to put on his clipboard. It really wasn't necessary and I had no idea how we would get it up there. Bud Beale's brother came by to chat and I told him what happened and I didn't know how we were going to get that dumb beam up. He laughed and said he thought he could help us. He engineered the whole thing, and the next thing I knew the steal beam was in place. It seemed that the Lord always sent the right man or the right material at the right time."

About 10 months after the first dirt was moved, the brand-new, spit-shined Portsmouth Alliance Church was ready for whatever God had in store for an excited Preacher and his equally eager church family. On Palm Sunday, 1962, the congregation met for the last time at the old church and sang a hymn. Then, escorted by a police motorcade with lights flashing and horns blowing, members drove their cars to the new church. Talk about a joyous ride. From a landing field for seagulls to a beautiful sanctuary, God had kept his promise as He always does. A new era in the life of the Portsmouth Alliance Church had begun.

Chapter 22

Growing And Expanding The Ministry

"And the Lord added to their number daily those who were being saved." **Acts 2:47 (NIV)**

It was early Monday morning and Preacher couldn't help but shed tears of joy. He had come by to marvel at the beautiful new church God had provided. The day before he had conducted the inaugural Palm Sunday service, and now he just wanted to spend a few quiet moments with his Lord. Standing in the back of the sanctuary, he saw through his mind's eye it being filled with people worshipping and singing praises to the almighty King of Kings. The church had been averaging around 175 people by the time the old church closed, and this new sanctuary would accommodate close to 500. Still, there was no doubt in his mind that someday they would need to open the two side wings, also known as the overflow rooms, located in the front to seat everyone. Looking at his watch and realizing he had visits to make, he slipped out of the church and made his way to his car.

As Preacher walked to the pulpit that Easter Sunday, he silently asked the Lord to bless the people he would be speaking to — his family. Taking his scripture text from the Gospels of Luke and Mark, he preached the message "Father Forgive Them."

"Jesus said, Father, forgive them, for they do not know what they are doing. And they divided up his clothes by casting lots." **Luke 23:34 (NIV)**

"It was the third hour when they crucified Him." **Mark 15:25 (NIV)**

Scanning the congregation, Preacher felt an overwhelming sense of gratitude for the love everyone in the church had shown he, Freda and the boys, and for their willingness to sacrifice so much to make the new church a reality. Never once did it occur to him the countless hours he had spent, often alone, in the mud and rain, working to see the dream of Rev. Harry Hardwick become a reality. Beginning his message, Preacher took his friends to a place on Mount Calvary where Jesus and two malefactors had been nailed to crude wooden crosses. There was a holy hush in the sanctuary as he repeated the words of Jesus, "Father forgive them." Then he reminded the congregation that this request by Jesus was all-inclusive. Seemingly looking at every individual in attendance square in the eye, Preacher told them that Jesus, while hanging on that cross, was talking directly to each of them and was asking His Father not to punish them and to blot out their sins. It was a truth Preacher would share with them many more times.

The following months were a whirlwind of activity at Alliance. The new church building drew curious visitors each week and the numbers — especially among children and young people — continued to multiply. One of the members who found herself with more "jobs" in the church than time was Delores Taylor who, with hands on hips, told Preacher one day she would not accept another single responsibility. She remembered him coming to her the very next week. "Don't you know he appeared at my door with a big bundle of Pioneer Club books. His words were something like 'Let's look at this and see if it will be good for our church.' So we looked the material over and decided it would be great to have the clubs for the growing mob of boys and girls in the church. When he walked out the door he left all the material on the table and told me to take my time getting the clubs organized, set up and running. I never had time to answer yes or no." Within six months, Alliance had its Pioneer Club for girls started and about a year later the Pioneer Boys were formed.

By the time fall 1962 rolled around it seemed like everyone in the church was involved doing something and Preacher loved every minute of it. Bob was finally a freshman at Cradock High School and had begun his career as a fullback, defensive end, punter and placekicker. Since Preacher had to pick him up after practice each day, he often came a little early to watch the team practice — just like he had done with Jim and Earl. Bob still cherishes those memories. "I would look up at practice and there he was, big as day, coat and tie. Dad always wore a tie and coat, unless it was really hot. Then just a tie. To him a preacher ought to look like a preacher. As the team chaplain, he never missed a Friday night game. Coach Weldon would talk to us before the game and then have us get on a knee as dad led us in prayer. I never once felt uncomfortable being the Preacher's son. I was a Christian and although I never felt the call to the ministry, I knew I wanted to be in God's will."

In early 1963 it was brought up that Preacher was still being paid by love offering. Sometimes he would "earn" as much as sixty dollars a week. But that "sometimes" didn't happen very often. At one of the monthly board meetings, the subject was brought up and one member suggested he reckoned it was time they put Preacher on a regular weekly salary. "He probably thought I was making too much money from the love offering, so he made a motion that they start paying me a weekly salary of one hundred dollars. Since on a real good Sunday the love offering might be as much as sixty dollars, I immediately seconded the motion. Man, that was quite a raise."

In February the Lord laid it on Preacher's heart to invite the church to open their hearts and their minds to that still small voice of God. Preacher believed there were so many voices out there in the world vying for people's time and attention. He chose an Old Testament scripture from I Samuel for this sermon and spoke on the subject of "Hearing the Voice of God."

"And the Lord came and stood there, calling as at the other times, Samuel! Samuel!

Then Samuel said, Speak, for your servant is listening." **I Samuel 3:10 (NIV)**

After reading the text, he enumerated many of the voices of sin in the word seeking to entrap each of them. He then challenged the congregation to open their hearts and ears to the working of the Holy Spirit, and urged them to spend time daily in Bible reading and prayer. Bringing his message to a close, Preacher asked the question: "Which voice will you listen to — the voice of the world or the voice of God?"

As spring erupted into a kaleidoscope of splendor, 16-year-old Jackie Beecher heard a rumor that the Portsmouth Alliance Church over on Portsmouth Boulevard was going to field a men's softball team. Although he had never played the sport before and had never attended Alliance, Beecher showed up for the first practice on the field behind the church. Someone told him to find the position he wanted to play, so he looked around to see which one had the least number of candidates. Beecher's eyes focused on second base, where only an older gentleman was standing. After a couple of ground balls somehow managed to make it through Beecher's legs, the older man half-heartedly gave him some advice on keeping his glove down. After another miss, he patted Beecher on the back and told him he probably didn't like second base anyhow and pointed him to the outfield. Second base still belonged to Preacher — bad knee and all. Beecher remained in the outfield that summer, and for the next few years played at nearby Alexander Baptist where he would become one of the fastest and most outstanding defensive players in the city if not the state. He eventually returned to Portsmouth Alliance and, in addition to being probably the best outfielder the church ever had, became a Sunday School teacher and elder.

Meanwhile, the old church and parsonage in Prentis Park had been sold to a new congregation. After several months living in a rental home on Elmhurst Lane, the governing board and congregation decided to build a parsonage on the back of the 10 or so acres of the church property, right where there had previously been a hog pen. This worked out perfectly for Preacher. There he could be separated from the church but still be on the property. Thanks to Roy Taylor, the home was built in 27 days at a cost of $15,000. God had once more provided for Pastor's needs.

Settled in his new home, Preacher continued to live a very busy life. In addition to preparing three sermons a week, visiting the sick and shut-ins, and various other "pastor" duties, he led the singing in the services, turned the lights and heat on and off before and after services, did a little cleaning up and generally served as friend and servant to everyone he met. Especially the young people — even though a few times they sorely tried his patience. Pam Sweeney Whitehurst remembered one such occasion. "One Sunday my parents were not in church and me, Linda Taylor and Wade Barker were sitting the back of the church talking away when all of a sudden Reverend Freeland stopped preaching and stared right back at the three of us. In no uncertain words, he told us to be quiet. I'll never forget that Sunday and you'd better believe it didn't happen again. I thanked the Lord that mom and dad were not there."

Not that every service went off without a hitch. Virginia Cuthriell and Chuck Conti both remembered a Sunday morning sermon Preacher delivered wearing one brown and one black shoe. Obviously Freda had failed to inspect him before he had left for church. The choir behind him were the only ones who noticed the two different shoes and, as hard as they tried, they couldn't keep from giggling. Preacher realized something was amiss and finally discovered the reason for all of their snickering. With a face as red as a fire engine, he continued his hell, fire and brimstone message without missing a beat.

The black shoe-brown shoe incident was barely history when, on a Sunday night, Preacher was again in high gear. Cuthriell was there that time, too. "Raising his voice, banging on the pulpit, face red with emotion, he yelled out to the congregation 'This world is a mess. It is just a big pot of mulligan stew. Do you know what mulligan stew is?' A holy hush fell over the whole congregation. Not a soul made a sound, dead silence filled the room. And then a little boy about midway back sitting with his parents reared up in his seat and said in a loud voice, 'No Preacher, what is it?' Preacher never finished the sermon. He laughed until he cried, stopped, started over, adjusted his tie, straightened his back, tried his best to regain his composure. To no avail. We all found out what mulligan stew was that night."

Preacher often threw in funny stories or perhaps a joke into his sermons. But make no mistake. When he was up on stage, you just knew God was standing there beside him. His son, Bob, summed it up best: "Dad had the ability to sense the moving of the Holy Spirit and sometimes after music he would give the altar call without ever preaching." Others, too, sensed the presence of the Holy Spirit in these services. I can personally recall several times when the convicting power of the Holy Spirit was so real, even at the beginning of the service, I whispered to my wife, Pris, that Rev. Freeland wouldn't be preaching that morning. On these occasions, he would simply give an altar call and people would respond.

Bob remembers how much he and his dad loved Sundays. Freda always got up early and prepared a full, delicious breakfast. While Bob and Preacher wiped their plates so clean they hardly needed washing, Freda would prepare most of the lunch meal before they left for Sunday School. That way she could have it on the table shortly after they got back home from church. And then came their favorite part. Not too long after finishing lunch, Preacher, Freda and Bob would all find a couch or chair and settle down for a Sunday afternoon nap. Lots of snoring, according to Bob. They would then get up and have a light snack, knowing they would be eating somewhere after the evening service. The Freelands always had fellowship with different church members on Sunday nights, either at a restaurant, another couple's home or at the parsonage. Preacher could think of no better way to close out the week.

As 1963 came to a close, Preacher chose the topic "Christmas Attitudes" finding his text in Matthew:

"After Jesus was born in Bethlehem in Judea, during the time of King Herod, Magi from the East came to Jerusalem and asked, Where is the one who has been born king of the Jews." **Matthew 2:1 (NIV)**

Preacher expanded the message far beyond the birth of the baby Jesus on that long ago Christmas morning. He told the congregation that in celebrating Christmas we too often fail to realize that the baby grew into manhood eventually becoming God's sacrifice on Calvary for the souls of men. Preacher closed by asking a pointed question to every person sitting there: "Have you found Him?"

Chapter 23

Around The World

"He said to them, Go into all the world and preach the good news to all creatures."
Mark 16:15 (NIV)

After the frenzied pace of Preacher's first four-and-a-half years in Portsmouth, 1964 was relatively calm — minus the fact that Bob had turned 16 and was now old enough to drive. Also, a young lady in the church, Kathy McCormick, had caught Bob's eye while traveling together to a Labor Day youth rally in Roanoke, VA. It wasn't long after they returned that the two started dating. Since there was only one car in the Freeland household, Bob had to ask ahead of time if he could use it to go out on a date. Preacher's answer was always the same: "You can use it if you can beat me three out of five." The Freelands had a ping-pong table out in the garage. If Bob wanted to borrow the car for a Friday night date, he first had to slam and volley his way past his dad — no easy accomplishment since Preacher hated to lose. Said Bob, "As I look back on those epic battles, I realize it was dad's way for us to spend some time together to do some bonding. He would always make sure we played long enough for me to get the edge. It brings back some awful good memories. Dad was strict but you always knew where he stood. We were not allowed to attend movies or go dancing, and through my high school years, curfew was eleven sharp. But it never occurred to me to break any of his rules. The most important thing to me was that I never to do anything to hurt or embarrass my dad."

Terri Sweeney Williams remembered one incident in 1964 that stuck with her for years. Just a little girl at the time, her dad, J.C. Sweeney, had given her a bag of Wonder Bread potato chips to share with the other kids in her Sunday School class. "Reverend Freeland, as he did so often, came into the class. Seeing the potato chips, he asked if he could try some. I told him I didn't have to share with him because my dad told me I was to share them with the other children in my class and he sure was no child. On that morning, Preacher called me "Termite" for the first time and the nickname has stuck with me all these years."

The Portsmouth Alliance Church continued to grow in numbers. Everywhere Preacher looked he saw children and teenagers, which pleased him to no end. And lo and behold, he even overheard some of the adults talking about the need for a fellowship hall and kitchen. He just smiled.

The first Sunday in December found Preacher in the pulpit taking about success and failure. He wanted to impress upon the congregation the importance of Jesus Christ as the answer to their every need. Using **John 5:5-9** as his text, he preached a dynamic sermon on "38 Years a Cripple."

"One who was there had been an invalid for thirty-eight years. When Jesus saw him lying there and learned that he had been in this condition for a long time, he asked him, Do you want to get well? Sir, the invalid replied, I have no one to help me into the pool when the water is stirred. While I am trying to get in, someone else goes down ahead of me." **John 5:5-9 (NIV)**

As he often did, Preacher painted a vivid word picture of the crippled man in his hopeless state, longing for a better life. He wanted to be whole. Then came the Master on the scene and finally the miracle. Preacher reminded the congregation that Jesus stands ready. That each and every one them holds the key to the entire success or failure of their lives — they only need to turn to Christ and plant their feet on the solid rock.

The talk of a new fellowship hall ceased to be a topic of conversation and a reality in September 1965. By now, motorists traveling along Portsmouth Boulevard were accustomed to seeing some kind of construction going on at the church. It was the third cornerstone in the Portsmouth Alliance Church complex, and provided a place where they could hold wedding receptions, dinners and other special events. In God's perfect scheduling, it was completed just in time for the annual missionary conference — the church's most anticipated event for that year. One of the guest speakers was to be Ed Jacober, a missionary from India, and Preacher could hardly wait to talk to him. While in college, he had felt he was being called to go to India as a missionary but God had other plans. Years later, Preacher would joke, "India did sound exciting, but I can just see me trying to speak whatever language they speak there."

During the missionary conference, Preacher found a sense of excitement welling up within him. Missions was an important part of the Portsmouth Alliance ministry and the annual pledge to support it had continued to go up each year. Jacober was an excellent speaker and that got Preacher fired up even more. Talking after one of the nightly services, Jacober casually told Preacher he should come visit him in India. He then baited him more by telling Preacher he would have the best guide in the entire country — himself. On a roll now, Jacober then suggested that instead of just a trip to India, Preacher should plan a trip around the world. Thinking the conversation was just chit-chat and no more than a far-fetched dream, Preacher forgot about it. But somebody from the church family had been listening in, and right after the conference was over, the congregation started taking up money to send Preacher on a missions trip.

Not knowing until the last minute he was actually going, Preacher had a myriad of details to work out. Building churches he knew, arranging an itinerary that would carry him more than halfway around the world not so much. He'd need to arrange to have a missionary meet him at every stop. He felt if he could get a first-hand feel what was happening on the missions field, he could be more effective back home in Portsmouth. The trials of organizing the trip would fill an entire book, but Preacher finally had what he hoped was a workable schedule ironed out. It was with the blessing of entire congregation that on November 29, traveling alone, Preacher embarked on his missionary trip of a lifetime.

The first leg of the journey took Preacher to Japan, where he knew Jon Conway. He was stationed in the military there and his father had lived in Japan for years as a successful businessman. Talk about eyes as big as saucers. Conway escorted Preacher all around the island nation, taking him to religious temples and other places he'd only seen in the pages of National Geographic. Preacher also took time to travel many miles to small villages so that he could acquaint himself with the customs of the people and manner in which they lived. Alliance only had a very small presence in Japan at the time, and it was the only country Rev. Freeland didn't preach in.

From there, Preacher traveled to Hong Kong where he spoke to a combined meeting of missionary groups from different denominations. More excitingly, he had the opportunity to preach several sermons on the rooftops of apartment buildings. "This was called rooftop evangelism. The apartments were built on blocks with no place for meeting except on the rooftop. There was a unique arrangement of classrooms on the roofs where children attended school in the daytime. Evening services brought an audience of a thousand or more, all of them who lived in the block apartments below." Preacher once again took time to visit 10 or so villages way on the outskirts where refugees from Red China lived in poverty much worse than anything he'd seen growing up in West Virginia.

Preacher's next stop was Saigon. Over the next week or so, he traveled over 2,300 miles carrying the evangelistic message to villages throughout South Vietnam. As he went into different villages and spoke to tribes like the Gari, Pleuiku and Raday, Preacher was keenly aware that the war in that country was very real. "We flew over the bombed areas and when on the ground could hear the anti-aircraft firing. The despair of the people was heartbreaking." Each day brought a new experience. Preacher remembered going into a village shortly after a funeral. "They had just buried the body and everybody was half-drunk with rice alcohol. Someone had a piece of pork in his hand and after rubbing it on his leg, handed it to me to eat. I declined as humbly as I knew how to. After the funeral, they laid the dead man's shield, a rice bowl and a couple of other articles next to the grave. They would come daily for one year and put rice and other food in the bowl. After that the grave site would be abandoned on the theory if he hadn't made friends in the afterlife by then, it was his problem. How these people needed the Lord."

In another village Preacher spoke in a small metal building where they held church services. He delivered his message through an interpreter, having no idea if what he was saying made sense or not. Preacher did remember those who came to the meeting seemed interested and he preached the simple Gospel as best he could, relying on God to nurture the seed.

Preacher remembered his next flight quite well. Flying in a missionary plane, he landed on a mountain top in the Sin Quang area of Laos. The short landing strip ran up the side of the mountain to help the pilot stop the plane in time. After arriving at the village, Preacher spoke through two interpreters, one for the Mao and one for the Laos tribes. After the message, the villagers prepared a special meal for Preacher and a missionary named Mr. Perkins, who had flown in with him. Preacher recognized it as chicken soup because it still had the feathers in it. As he spoke in other nearby villages, the practice of serving him a "special" dinner continued. "In one village they served something that looked like a cauliflower. I took a big bite and it squished in my mouth. I looked over at the missionary who was accompanying me and he was laughing with tears in his eyes. Then he told me I was eating fish lungs. Didn't matter to me. If they could eat it, so could I. But thinking about it, I don't remember any of the natives eating that stuff that night."

Leaving Laos, Preacher and several missionaries traveled by car to Bangkok, Thailand, where he had the privilege of speaking at the only Leper Bible College in the world. The students, often with hands and fingers that were mere nubs, leafed through their Bibles as he preached through an interpreter the word of God. Preacher remembered speaking to and praying with those precious people as being one of the real highlights of the trip.

Thankfully, the next leg of Preacher's odyssey took him by commercial flight to India, where he was met by Rev. and Mrs. Jacober. They accompanied Preacher on all his travels there, including a visit to a village where no one had ever heard of Jesus or the Christian religion. Preacher had been invited only because the parents of a little boy in the village had received much-needed medical treatment thanks to the Jacobers. That act was their ticket into the village, which normally would have been off limits because of the caste system. The trip to the isolated village was eventful in its own right. The first part was taken in an old Chevrolet the Jacober's owned, which kept running hot and requiring water. The last five hours were by ox cart. Once finally there, they handed out tracts and Mrs. Jacober was allowed to teach a Sunday School lesson in their native language. The food served at the boy's home was another experience, but Preacher found it to be delicious and had a second helping. The tea — made of boiled goat's milk mixed with spices and sugar syrup — was another matter.

At another village Preacher spoke beneath a Ban-ion tree, whose branches grow sideways and sprout down into the ground forming a natural building. One of the few converts to Christianity there fixed a native meal that was so hot Preacher described it as sticking fire in his mouth. The two became quick friends, and before Preacher left, the man presented him with a gift of nuts and fruit that he had carved from wood.

As he visited different places in India and saw first-hand the heathen practices, Preacher's heart went out to the people. They worshipped thousands of different gods, none of which could satisfy the longing in their hearts. Preacher left there with a real understanding of the trials Alliance missionaries endured in India and a profound admiration for those called to serve there.

And then finally it was off to the Holy Land, the last stop in Preacher's whirlwind tour. He elected not to use a guide there, preferring to walk through the life of Christ alone. In Bethany he visited the grave site of Lazarus. He then made his way to nearby Jerusalem and to the Garden Tomb where many believe Jesus was buried. Preacher climbed the hill to Calvary, picturing in his mind his Savior hanging on the cross. In Bethlehem, he walked underneath the Church of the Nativity, thought to be built over the stable where the Christ child was born. Walking through the gardens nearby, he met an old gardner who gave him some seeds from a flower. Preacher put them in his pocket thinking he would plant them when he got back home. Continuing on, he strolled through the gates of the city and up Mount Olive. "That morning there was a kindred scene like a rainbow. Tears streamed down my face and I thought He's coming again, and His feet are going to land right here. As I was walking up the mountain a little boy came up and started walking with me. He reached in a bag he was carrying and handed me an orange. He spoke a little English and we walked a long way together." As Preacher continued his tour, the Bible seemed to jump out at him. Bethlehem. Capernaum. It was very possible, he thought, that he was walking on the same path Jesus walked nearly 2,000 years before. Preacher also visited the pool at Siloam, the Sea of Galilee and the Jordan River. At each site, he would close his eyes and see his Lord — standing in a boat, healing the sick, instructing his disciples and teaching the multitudes.

During his visit, Preacher was blessed to be asked to speak on two occasions. In Israel he spoke at the Alliance Church in Beersheba and on Christmas Eve he delivered a short sermon in the "Shepherds Field" near Bethlehem in Jordan where the Wise Men are said to have heard the message of the Savior's birth.

The trip had a profound impact on Preacher's ministry. "What a glorious time and I thanked the Lord over and over for allowing me to visit the very area where my Savior was born, ministered, died and rose. You can't paint a picture if you haven't seen it." On the flight home, Preacher remembered the seeds from the garden and the regulation against bringing back anything like that into the United States. He flushed them in the plane toilet and prayed they landed somewhere and grew. He also wondered if there was sermon topic mixed in with those seeds. Preacher arrived back at the Norfolk (VA) Airport late Wednesday night, January 6, 1966, and was greeted by Freda, Bob and 75 church members. Preacher was home and Dick Thompson, who had filled the pulpit for him while he was gone, thanked God the most.

Chapter 24

Young People Everywhere

"Remember your Creator in the days of your youth, before the days of trouble come and the years approach when you say, I find no pleasure in them."
Ecclesiastes 12:1 (NIV)

In early 1966 Preacher received a call from Mr. Booker, principal of Cradock High School. Before he had left on his missions trip, the school and football team had honored Preacher for his years of service as chaplain. Since Bob would be graduating in June, it was assumed Preacher had "retired" now that he didn't have any more kids coming through the football program. Mister Booker called to ask Preacher if he would consider continuing as team chaplain, which he gladly agreed to. During the conversation they discussed Preacher's trip around the world and Booker wondered if he would also like to share his experiences and slides to the entire student body. Over the next two weeks, Preacher spoke six times at special chapels in the school's auditorium. Preacher was in his element. "I had taken hundreds of slides and shared them with the entire student body at Cradock. I was never restricted in what I could say. Seizing the opportunity, I talked to those young students straight out about the Lord and what He was doing around the world. I always wondered if somewhere down the line one of those kids became a missionary."

Back in his own church, Preacher couldn't help but notice the large number of young people on Sunday mornings. The back rows were filled with them. With the new fellowship hall complete, Preacher believed Portsmouth Alliance had the perfect place where all those children and young people could go to have fun. Henry Neal, who was later to become a church elder and be in charge of the visitation ministry for the church (and the father-in-law of my son, Bud Jr.), was the volunteer youth director with plenty of help from his wife Edna, Virginia Cuthriell, Delores Taylor and many others. They got together and decided is would be a great idea to open the fellowship hall to the kids on Saturday night. A ping-pong table, shuffleboard and other games were brought in. Cuthriell knew the folks at Poffenberger's Bakery nearby and on Saturday afternoon all of the leftover items would wind up in the fellowship hall. Saturday night became a weekly highlight for the youth and with all those delicious buns and pastries, there was never a shortage of adult supervision. Including Preacher.

Every night before going to sleep, Preacher would thank the Lord for what He was doing in his church. "I never stopped thanking Him for using an old coal miner like me. You know, the Lord knew from the day he called me to the ministry that I didn't feel worthy. He and I got that part straight walking down the road that day, and I never lost sight of the fact that I could do nothing but allow Him to work in my life as He saw fit."

Right in the middle of a busy year, Bob graduated from Cradock and started making plans to attend nearby Old Dominion University in Norfolk. He would still be living at home and the only real concession Preacher made was to extend his curfew to eleven thirty. And he still had to beat his dad three of out five to use the car to date Kathy McCormick.

In early June, while studying and praying about a message for the following Sunday morning service, Preacher was led to **Mark 10:46-52** where it talked about Jesus healing the blind man. He then quickly sketched out a message of hope to the many who were blind in their sin and would be among his congregation.

"Then they came to Jericho. As Jesus and his disciples, together with a large crowd, were leaving the city, a blind man, Bartimaeus (that is, the Son of Timaeus), was sitting by the roadside begging. When he heard that it was Jesus of Nazareth, he began to shout, Jesus, Son of David, have mercy on me. Many rebuked him and told him to be quiet, but he shouted all the more, Son of David, have mercy on me! Jesus stopped and said, Call him. So they called to the blind man, Cheer up! On your feet! He's calling you. Throwing his cloak aside, he jumped to his feet and came to Jesus. What do you want me to do for you? Jesus asked him. The blind man said, Rabbi, I want to see. Go, said Jesus, your faith has healed you. Immediately he received his sight and followed Jesus along the road." **Mark 10:46-52 (NIV)**

That Sunday, Preacher took his church family on a road trip from Jericho to Jerusalem that had happened the week before Calvary. They listened as Preacher described the shouting multitudes, many who were poor and sick, cry out to Jesus: "Heal me, feed me, give me money, take me home." He then invited the congregation to hear one cry that was above all others: "Jesus, thou son of David, have mercy on me." Preacher then identified five things about this man with the loud voice: He was in darkness; was destitute; was drawn; was delivered; and became devoted. As sermon drew to a close, Preacher asked everybody to recognize their own blindness and let Jesus meet their every need.

The next six months moved quickly and before he knew it, Preacher was preparing another Christmas message. This time he went to a Psalm for his reading and chose as his title "What Did You Get for Christmas?"

"Delight yourself in the Lord and he will give you the desires of your heart. Commit your way to the Lord; trust in him and he will do this." **Psalm 37:4-5 (NIV)**

Preacher began the sermon by recalling some of the many gifts Jesus gave during his ministry on earth — how he caused the lame man to walk, the blind to see, the man with palsy to be healed, Lazarus to be returned to the living, the hungry to be fed, and several other examples. Pausing for a moment, he then told the congregation the greatest gift Jesus gave was His life. He closed with the words, "He who has not Christmas in his heart will not find it under a tree."

As 1966 bowed gracefully from the stage, Jean Davis, organist, pianist and choir member, composed a beautiful poem about Preacher entitled *"Just You."* It was a fitting tribute to end one year and wander into the next.

Chapter 25

And Now A School

"After three days they found him in the temple courts, sitting among the teachers, listening to them and asking them questions." **Luke 2:46 (NIV)**

Here's a message for all you young married couples — and especially the husbands — out there. You can forget your best friend's name from elementary school, your social security number and even taking out the garbage occasionally. What you can't afford to forget is your anniversary. Around April or May 1967, it dawned on Preacher that this was a very important year... the 25th anniversary of the Portsmouth Alliance Church. And he hadn't even needed Freda to remind him. Figuring it was never too early to start preparing, he marked Sunday, September 24, 1967, on the calendar as the celebration date.

Meanwhile, his son Bob was finishing his first year at Old Dominion University and having doubts about returning for his sophomore year. He was anxious to earn some money, missed playing football, and perhaps more importantly, thinking about having to wait three more years before he could marry Kathy McCormick. Hearing about the Apprentice School program at the Newport News (VA) Shipbuilding and Drydock Co., he realized that might be the answer. He could get a great education while earning a regular paycheck and play football, to boot. The Apprentice School had a fine football program and routinely played small college and junior college teams. Bob applied and was accepted for the fall term.

Over in Suffolk, Eddie Mitchell was finishing school at Frederick College. Mitchell, who would later become a church leader and elder at Portsmouth Alliance, remembered meeting Preacher there the first time. "There was required Sunday night chapel at Frederick and different local pastors would speak to the student body. Reverend Freeland was the speaker at one of the chapels and quite a few students accepted the Lord as the Savior that evening. Of all the chapels I attended that was the only time students were saved."

The 25th anniversary celebration was a joyous occasion. Doctor L.L. King, Foreign Secretary of the Christian & Missionary Alliance, was invited to be the guest speaker at both the morning and evening worship services. After Preacher led the congregation in two great hymns — *"All Hail the Power"* and *"Great is Thy Faithfulness,"* Dr. King delivered a ringing message that morning. The evening service climaxed a great day for the church. In addition to another inspiring message by Dr. King and comments on the history of the Portsmouth Alliance Church by Mrs. Caswell, Preacher took the opportunity to remind the congregation of some of the future goals that had been listed in the church bulletin that morning. Among the objectives — which included continuing to win souls for Christ, encouraging and trusting God and installing carpeting in the sanctuary — was a line that drew little notice: Put the remainder of our property to better use. Not even Preacher had thought much about it and he'd been the one who helped come up with the list.

In addition to the church's anniversary, the fall turned out to be, as usual, a busy time for the Freelands. Bob was now enrolled in the Apprentice School and playing fullback, outside linebacker and punter. Those of you keeping score at home will be glad to know the next summer, he and Kathy were finally married. He would finish the program in 1971, the same year his first son, Bobby, was born. Anyhow, the fall of 1967 found Preacher back on familiar ground, pacing the sidelines at Cradock High School as the football team's chaplain. He and Coach Larry Weldon had become close friends and spent many hour's on Weldon's boat fishing for blue gill and talking about the Lord. In addition to Weldon, Preacher got to know Alvin Anderson, a teacher at Cradock and devout Christian. They often talked about the Lord and at some point Anderson and his wife started attending Alliance.

During conversations between the three, Weldon often opined he thought it might be about time for him to get out of teaching and coaching. He'd been doing it for 20 years and no longer felt he had the authority or backing to discipline his students. He cited examples of kids coming into the classroom, putting their heads on the desk and sleeping with no fear of punishment. As Preacher listened, he noticed that Anderson shook his head in agreement at everything Weldon was saying.

As the weeks went by, Preacher often thought about that conversation and worried about the young people of the city. Other times, and for no apparent reason, he would reflect on one of the "minor" goals set forth during the 25th anniversary — to better utilize the remaining church property. But he never connected the two... or at least not yet.

Anderson also started thinking about the conversation. In talking to some local educators he discovered there were a couple of private Christian grade schools in the area, but none that carried all the way through high school. It wasn't long before Anderson approached Preacher with the idea of starting a Christian high school at Portsmouth Alliance. Preacher's immediate reaction was to tell Anderson he was out of his mind. "In ministerial meetings I attended there was some talk of Christian schools. There were two local grade schools and they felt if there was a Christian high school in the area they could funnel their kids to that school. Being the only paid employee for the church with more than enough of a load, I dismissed any idea of our church becoming involved."

The conversation with Anderson had taken place during the early part of 1968. Later on that year while seeking the will of God for a Sunday sermon, Preacher found himself reading a scripture from **I Thessalonians 2:18**: *"For we wanted to* come to you — certainly I, Paul, did, again and again. But Satan stopped us." As he bowed his head in prayer, God confirmed this was to be the message he would preach. As he scribbled his thoughts on the back of a sheet of church stationary, he jotted down six things Satan tries to hinder us from: worship, prayer, praise, thanksgiving, communion and witnessing. And then he wrote the following thought: "You are the key to unlock someone's life. Witness to His mercy, His love and His Power."

As he sat at his office desk, Anderson and the conversation about starting a Christian high school came to mind. As he looked back at his notes, all Preacher could see were the words "witnessing" and "You are the key to unlock someone's life." After composing himself, he continued preparing for his Sunday sermon, but something told him God had something really big in mind for the church.

The early months of 1969 were reasonably quiet around the Portsmouth Alliance Church, at least for Preacher. For one thing, Chuck Conti had finally agreed to become the song leader. Preacher laughed to himself, thinking he must be getting lazy in his old years to let young Chuck, the singing mechanic, take his spot. Still, there was that nagging thought in the back of his mind that there was simply way too much vacant land on the church property. Seemed a shame to let it just sit there unused. He'd read enough scriptures to know if you left fruit lying around for a long period of time it would go bad. Laughing at himself once more, Preacher wondered if vacant land ever went bad and if maybe there was sermon in there somewhere. Although he didn't see a direct connection, he thought of a sermon he had preached many years before in Clearfield, PA, about "Barn Builders." Digging through thousands of notes from previous sermons, he found that in October 1959 he had preached that sermon to his congregation from the Gospel of Luke:

"And He told them this parable: The ground of a certain rich man produced a good crop. He thought to himself, What shall I do? I have no place to store my crops. Then he said, This is what I'll do. I will tear down my barns and build bigger ones, and there I will store all my grain and my goods. And I'll say to myself, You have plenty of good things laid up for many years. Take life easy; eat, drink and be merry. But God said to him, You fool! This very night your life will be demanded of you. Then who will get what you have prepared for yourself? This is how it will be with anyone who stores up things for himself but is not rich toward God." **Luke 12:16-21 (NIV)**

Scanning the outline he was reminded that he had told his church family back then: "God gives us our todays to get us ready for His tomorrows." He had then challenged them to look through the barns of their life and find out what they were filled with, and throw out the bad stuff and use the good stuff. As he had been doing a lot lately, Preacher wondered if God was preparing he and the church for an even greater ministry in Portsmouth. He preached that sermon the following Sunday.

As spring 1970 dared peak her color-ladened head around the corner, the people at the Portsmouth Alliance Church prepared for another great year. So did the men's softball team which by now had become pretty good. And though Preacher had "retired" from the active roster, he never missed a game and could be heard rooting on the younger guys and needling the older ones. J.C. Sweeney, who would become an elder and trustee in the church, was on that team. "I remember in one I was on third base and headed for home. I stumbled and fell flat on my embarrassment, looking up to see home plate staring me in the face. I started to crawl when a voice I had heard so many times from the pulpit yelled out, 'Here comes twinkle toes.' Wouldn't you know that the next Sunday morning he called on 'Twinkle toes, oh I mean J.C.' to pray."

In early fall Preacher and Anderson had another long conversation. He and Coach Weldon had both left Cradock High School. Anderson was working with Nansemond-Suffolk Academy, a relatively new private school that had opened in 1966 on the outskirts of town, setting up the curriculum. Anderson had established a Bible class at the school and Preacher would come and teach the class. At lunch one day, Anderson again brought up the subject of a Christian high school for Portsmouth and asked Preacher if he had thought any more about it. "I told him, Alvin, we don't have a penny to start a school — nothing. How in the world could we ever start a school." Anderson then looked Preacher in the eye and asked him if he had prayed about it. Feeling his neck getting red, he admitted he had not.

Back in his office, Anderson's question about praying whether Portsmouth Alliance should open a high school continued to nag at Preacher. Then the sermon about barn building came racing back into his thoughts. From its humble beginning on Des Moines Avenue, the Lord had seen fit to give them 10 or so acres and a beautiful new church, parsonage and fellowship hall. Should they be content or was it time to go out again on faith? Since it was such a beautiful day, Preacher decided to wander back home and spend some time on the front porch.

It was a lazy fall afternoon and the leaves from all those trees were just starting to fall. June was sitting on the front porch of his home enjoying the million or so squirrels, birds, cats, dogs and other unidentified animals as they paraded by. Of course, it wasn't his home by legal definition but the parsonage of the Portsmouth Christian & Missionary Alliance Church. And the only person this side of West Virginia who knew him by "June" was his wife, Freda. To the multitude of people in Portsmouth who knew and loved him he was Pastor Earl Freeland or most often simply "Preacher." And this afternoon Preacher was doing what he'd done as often as possible since 1963, when the church built the house on the back side of the church property. He was looking over the 10 or so acres of church property and the magnificent church the Lord had blessed the congregation with. Preacher closed his eyes and leaned back. It was impossible to tell whether he was dreaming or just remembering.

He had been the pastor at three churches in Pennsylvania before God told him to come to Portsmouth and build a church. Seemed like every time he had gotten comfortable there was that small voice and it usually meant one of three things — move, renovate or build. This afternoon Preacher was confident in his own mind those days were over. He was certain he was in God's will in Portsmouth. The church and fellowship hall were a perfect fit for the congregation. All was well. He would serve the church as long as God wanted him there. And then he would retire. A serene nap was interrupted by the barking of a hound chasing a squirrel, causing him to sit up and again look over the property. Seemed to him it was an awful lot of land for just a church, fellowship hall and ranch home. And then, the tap on his shoulder. As he looked across the property he heard something. Not the chirping of birds or the bark of that ole' hound dog. No, it was the sound of a bouncing basketball. Here we go again, he thought. Time to build a school.

As he prayed, Preacher put out a fleece. "I said Lord, if you really want me to start a school, you have to show me." Unknown to him, Anderson had already made inquiries about some desks he heard were available and mentioned the Portsmouth Alliance Church might be interested. It wasn't many days later that Preacher received a call from a man he had never heard of asking if the church needed some school desks. "I hadn't said a word about the school, even to my wife, and I almost dropped the phone. I stuttered and stammered around and finally asked the man how much he wanted for the desks. When he said fifty cents each I told him to hold on to them and I would get back with him."

Meanwhile, the Lord continued working through Anderson. He had purchased a library of books from Ft. Meade Army Base in Maryland for 10 cents each and decided to use the collection as "evidence" on Preacher. When he approached a few weeks later with the offer of a "ready-made" library, Preacher was so overjoyed he immediately called and bought the desks. Preacher remembered it as being like a runaway train. "There we were, library and desks but no school to put them in. Not only that, I hadn't even talked to the church board about the school. I had mentioned it to the ole' dog, assorted squirrels and rabbits, a few birds and countless other animals wandering around the parsonage, but reckoned that probably didn't count. When I finally got up enough nerve to talk to the board they were reluctant and said it was a matter that would have to be brought before the entire church family. I said fine, if this is what the Lord wants we're probably going to have to do it." After a lot of prayer and a few more afternoons sitting on his porch, Preacher presented the idea to the congregation. He was filled with a sense of thanks when everyone seemed receptive to the concept of a high school as a ministry of the church. When the desks arrived, the ladies of the church refinished them and they looked brand new. This was the beginning of the church's involvement. It was then decided they would use the upstairs of the church for classrooms and the fellowship hall for the cafeteria. Then they started making plans to find a faculty and students. Finally, it was determined that the first class would be introduced in September 1971 — the very next fall. Nothing to it, Preacher thought. If God could make the blind man see and the lame man walk, He certainly could rise up a school in nine or 10 months.

Chapter 26

Busy Days

"Surely He has done great things." **Joel 2:20 (NIV)**

The reality of bringing a Christian high school to life boggled Preacher's mind. Here he was, the only paid employee of a growing church, taking on another new project. But he loved it. By early 1971 it was obvious to him and the people of the Portsmouth Alliance Church that God had future plans for all that vacant property. He'd been talking about the school with his congregation for a few months but, as the old saying goes, "talk is cheap" and it was time to get going. As much to encourage himself as his congregation, Preacher delivered a Sunday morning message preparing them for the task ahead — one that would require a unified church and another miracle or two from the Lord. Fortunately, most of the church family there that day had already been through the experience of building a church, parsonage and fellowship hall. They welcomed the challenge. He preached his sermon from James and entitled it "Faithful Trees."

"Everyone should be quick to listen, slow to speak and slow to become angry... Do not merely listen to the word, and so deceive yourselves. Do what it says."
James 1:19&22 (NIV)

After he spoke of the admonition Christians have to not just be hearers but also doers of the Word, Preacher advised them to go home and get out their hammers, saws and other tools because there were young people throughout the city who needed a high school where they could get a quality education in a Christian environment.

Alvin Anderson agreed to be the first principal, and immediately went to work setting up the school's curriculum and plowing through all the administrative details. Shortly before accepting the job, he had been offered a high-paying position setting up the school curriculum for the state of West Virginia. After much prayer and with the support of his family, he declined the offer so he could fully commit to the soon-to-be Alliance Christian High School. Finding other faculty members proved to be more difficult. Preacher used all of his people skills to convince prospective staff members and teachers that it was going to be the finest Christian high school in Portsmouth. Of course, he forgot or neglected to tell them it would be the only one. He remembered having to pull out all the strings to convince one lady in particular to accept the cafeteria manager's position. After telling her she was the best cook he had ever known, Freda finally accepted.

Everything appeared to be in order as the first day of school approached. That is, until Preacher remembered the bouncing basketball. Hammer in hand, he went out and nailed a backboard and rim on the telephone pole behind the church. He chuckled to himself and wondered if Alliance would be selected to host the private school state basketball championships that year.

And finally — or way too quickly, depending on which student or teacher you asked — the first day of school arrived. Preacher had volunteered to teach mechanical drawing and announced to Roy Taylor and anyone else who would listen that he was now a full-fledged educator. As the students arrived, he couldn't keep a tear or two or maybe a million from running down the side of his face. God had provided another miracle. Tim Lane was in the inaugural class and remembered, fondly, some of the sacrifices the students had to make. "We had classes in the church and for some reason I remember they had nailed a blackboard on the wall. Certainly wasn't fancy. We didn't have a gym and there were no organized sports. There was a metal shed behind the fellowship hall that housed the tractor used to cut the grass. We would go outside in the vacant field for gym and naturally get dirty and sweaty. With no place to take a shower, we all suffered the rest of the day. Not to worry. We pulled the tractor out of the shed, threw a tarp over it, and after running a garden hose into the shed had our own shower. We had an old school bus but keeping it running was a challenge and more often than not when we were going someplace we had to borrow a blue bus from Bethany Baptist. We named her 'old blue.'"

Space was tight and there were many occasions when something would get broken. That's when Earnest Knox would step in. He worked in maintenance at Virginia Chemical Corp., and was good at fixing things. He had been a member since 1944 and acted as the handy man. When it was decided to put the school library in the sanctuary balcony, he built the needed rails to keep everybody safe. But his best talent was in how quick he could work. If he saw something broken, he would fix it immediately so no one in the church would be upset with the school.

Bev McNeal was the unpaid treasurer and bookkeeper that first year. She remembered lunch time always being an adventure. "We would have our lunch in the cafeteria together; teachers, staff and students. It didn't take me long to figure out that if you wanted to keep your lunch from the mischievousness of Preacher you better not turn your back on it. He would either hide your plate or 'doctor' up your food with hot sauce and then sit there looking so innocent when you returned."

McNeal also remembered the time several years later when Preacher almost got the school in hot water with the Internal Revenue Service. She had filled out the IRS forms of declaration as to the school's tax-exempt status, put them in a stamped envelope with the IRS address typed on it, and then told Preacher all he had to do was sign it and "file" it. She didn't realize until later Preacher didn't understand that term. "I kept receiving IRS notices that they had not received the form. I ignored the first two notices, but after the third one I asked the church secretary if I could rummage through Preacher's files just to make sure. And there it was, the stamped and addressed envelope still attached with a paper clip. I sent a cover letter with the form to the IRS explaining what had happened. I hope it gave one of the humorless agents a good laugh."

It was also McNeal's young daughter, Laurie, who discovered Preacher wasn't perfect, just saved. McNeal remembered it this way. "Laurie stayed with the Freelands when my husband and I took a business trip to Chicago. She loved both of them to death. After we got back Laurie commented, "Boy, Preacher sure is grumpy before he gets his morning coffee. We had a big laugh over that chink in the armor."

Finances were as tight as a pair of shoes three sizes too small that first year but the school survived and even added several new students as the year progressed. Anderson didn't receive a salary for the first four months and then settled on $50 a week. McNeal and Mary Buhls, the school secretary, worked for free, as did Freda and her cafeteria staff. To make up for the lack of pay, Preacher complimented them almost every day. "Cheap labor, huh? But they were good. Freda made a mean pot of goulash."

By the end of the first school year Alliance Christian had an enrollment of 37 students. As soon as the last bell rang marking the beginning of summer break, Anderson and Preacher met to discuss the highs and lows. Both agreed God had really blessed them. But they also knew they would need to begin the process of building an educational facility for the school to have a meaningful impact on the community.

But first he needed a break. With all the evening and weekend activities of the church plus school during the day, Preacher sometimes felt like he was meeting himself coming and going. For the first time he could remember, he felt just a tinge of weariness. He'd been going full speed ahead the past several years and his 53-year-old bones could feel it. After someone reminded him he had vacation time he really should take, Preacher decided to take a few days in late July to do some deep sea fishing off the Outer Banks of North Carolina. Aboard the fishing boat *Sportsman*, he hooked and boated an award-winning white marlin and, after having his picture taken with the fish, released it back into the Gulf Stream. He couldn't wait to get back in the pulpit and brag about another "fish" that hadn't got away.

Feeling strengthened and renewed, Preacher barely had time to get his coat and tie on when it was time to start hiring teachers for the second year and preparing for the August 14, 1972, groundbreaking for the new school building. One of those he interviewed and hired was Caroline Pond, a young lady who applied for a teaching position in the Phys Ed Department. "I am sure God sent me to the Alliance Christian School to teach and have Reverend and Mrs. Freeland greatly influence my life in a positive way. While shopping with my mom I bought two plaques, one of which stayed in my home and one that stayed in Reverend Freeland's study. The plaques read 'You never fail until you stop trying' and I was honored to think he would put it with his important things." Pond became a fixture at the school.

Groundbreaking finally arrived with much fanfare and a healthy dose of nervous anticipation. After all, this was a huge step of faith. Most of the church members and scores of friends joined teachers, staff and a whopping 92 students at the ceremony. Jack Barnes, Mayor of the city of Portsmouth, officiated the event and later watched his daughter graduate from Alliance Christian School. Standing next to Barnes, Preacher leaned over and whispered in his ear, "Be real quiet Mr. Mayor and if you listen real hard you can hear children laughing, teachers teaching and, oh yeah, the bouncing of a basketball." Looking at the backboard nailed to the telephone pole, Preacher could feel his chest expanding and thought he could see a beautiful basketball court rising.

Mitchell Engineering was contracted to build a gymnasium and six classrooms separate from the church and fellowship hall. The goal was to have the project completed by the end of Christmas break. One day during construction a welder failed to show up, threatening an already tight schedule. Preacher went home, changed his clothes, returned and did the job himself. Once again, the skills he had learned before becoming a Christian and being led into the ministry had paid off.

While Preacher "supervised" the construction, Anderson was busy working out the details of the second year of classes. He wrote a personal letter to each family who would have a son or daughter in the school, welcoming them to the Alliance family and, ever so gently, urging them to pay the tuition fee by August 25, 1972. He followed this up with another letter inviting them to a parents' meeting scheduled for August 29. He also mentioned that the school bus which had been ordered would not be available until October and temporary arrangements were being made. The fellowship hall was filled with parents anxious for the school year to begin.

Anderson and Preacher met one more time to make sure everything was in order. They knew this would be a critical year in the life of the school, and both were determined to make it go as smoothly as possible. After prayer, they reviewed the background and experience of the teachers and were satisfied God had sent the right people for the right jobs. And though space was tighter than ever, the first few months flew by and even the school bus they had ordered rolled onto the parking lot a few days ahead of schedule. Still, staff, teachers and students, alike, were ecstatic to move into the "real" school building right before Christmas as planned.

Everything about the new school building was perfect in Preacher's eyes. For about a minute. That's when students started showing up in the office with scraped knees, elbows and assorted other body parts. They had put down a concrete floor in the gymnasium and somehow nobody had foreseen the carnage it would cause. Told that a parquet floor (Preacher probably envisioned the Boston Garden where the NBA Celtics played) would solve the problem, the school agreed to pay $4,000 to have one installed. Here's how Preacher recalled the investment: "When they laid the floor they didn't clean the concrete and within a couple of weeks it looked like prairie dogs had built houses on the floor. Talk about a buckled floor. It would even buckle up while the kids were playing. Somebody, mostly me, had to take case-hardened nails and go out and nail that dumb thing back down." The school sued and got its money back, and Charlie Johnson, a local builder, agreed to put in a real maple floor. To this day, Alliance Christian still has one of the finest wooden gym floors of any school in the Tidewater area — public or private. And since there were no bleachers, Preacher and church member Danny Holland decided they would build some, doing all the welding themselves. Years later, when the school was able to install professional fold-away bleachers, the "home-made" ones were carried out to the baseball field where they, too, still proudly serve.

With the close of the 1972-73 school year, Alliance Christian School celebrated the graduation of its first six students. Richard Clark, Hubert (Bud) Conner, Jr., Pamela House, William Powell, Pearl Stallings and Thomas Walker, Jr., would be just the first of many who would follow.

Chapter 27

Roots And Wings

"But those who hope in the Lord will renew their strength. They will soar on wings like eagles; they will run and not grow weary; they will walk and not be faint."
Isaiah 40:31 (NIV)

Like a mighty oak, the Alliance church had been sinking deep roots in Portsmouth since 1942. From humble beginnings the church had been faithful to the calling to "Go and preach the Gospel" and God had blessed in so many ways. With over 10 acres of land now adorned with a beautiful church, fellowship hall, parsonage and Christian high school, it stood out as a lighthouse for so many people — people who came to worship and grow as Christians; people drawn by the opportunity to have children receive a quality education in a Christian setting; and people tired of a life of sin and wanting to turn their lives over to Christ. The ministry of the church and school was meeting their needs. A few people like Virginia Cuthriell had been with the church since its inception and many others had worshipped in the church for years. Others had only recently joined the fellowship. And then there were the precious young people in the school who had been adopted as part of the church family. The church accepted everyone and turned no one away. And finally there was Rev. Freeland. You'd have a hard time finding anybody in Portsmouth or even the surrounding cities who didn't know Preacher.

During the early part of 1974 Preacher used the words "Adopted" and "Accepted" as message topics during two Sunday morning services. He wanted all who heard the sermons to know with complete assurance that no matter the mess they had made of their lives, God still wanted them to become a part of His family — just like the Portsmouth Alliance Church wanted them to become a part of its family. For first sermon, "Adopted," he took as his scripture from Romans:

"Because those who are led by the Spirit of God are sons of God. For you did not receive a spirit that makes you a slave again to fear, but you received the Spirit of sonship. And by him we cry Abba, Father. The Spirit himself testifies with our spirit that we are God's children. Now if we are children, then we are heirs — heirs of God and co-heirs with Christ, if indeed we share in his sufferings in order that we may also share in his glory." **Romans 8:14-17**

Preacher reminded the congregation that God chose them to be a member of His family and that they have access to Him, a home in heaven, and an inheritance. He then invited those who did not know the Lord as their personal Savior to turn to Him who alone is their salvation.

The second sermon, "Accepted," was lifted from Ephesians:
"To the praise of his glorious grace, which he has freely given us in the One he loves." **Ephesians 1:6 (NIV)**

Preacher proclaimed that although we have sinned by word, deed, thought, commission and omission, there is one who still cares and who will accept us as His very own. Though our hands have sinned (**James 4:8**); though our ears have sinned (**Mark 8:18**); though our tongue has sinned (**Psalm 140:3**); and though our eyes lust (**I John 2:16**), there is still hope. All we have to do is turn to **John 3:16** and believe.

"For God so loved the world that he gave his one and only Son, that whoever believes in him shall not perish but have eternal life." **John 3:16 (NIV)**

The 1973-74 school year at Alliance began on a sad note when Alvin Anderson, co-founder and principal the first two years, announced during the summer he was leaving to pursue his doctorate at the University of Virginia in Charlottesville. Convinced the school was on solid footing, he recommended that Nell Richardson be named the new principal. She had done an outstanding job teaching math and serving as guidance counselor. Preacher agreed. On a bright note, the school had 97 students enrolled and chorus, under the direction of new teacher Bernice Verbyla, would be offered for the first time. Preacher knew how important music was in his church services, and was thrilled the school would now be able to nurture a new generation of talented singers to praise the Lord. Momentum continued the next school year and when fall classes began, you could hear Preacher shouting from the rooftops. He had waited upon the Lord for a school enrollment of 100 and he had sent them 102 by the time classes started.

Preacher continued to make monumental impacts on the people he met. Everywhere he went — and he went most everywhere — he sought out people who were hurting and brought a little sunshine into their dark, gloomy days. Young people were his speciality and they were immediately attracted to his mile-wide smile and gift of making people laugh, oftentimes at their own expense.

One of these young people was Steve Minter. "As a ten or eleven-year-old I spent most of my Saturday nights in the Alliance gym watching my dad's team, Alexander Baptist, in the church recreational league. I fondly remember the small concession stand and a friendly gentleman who knew lots of magic tricks. Oven evening he showed me a hidden quarter trick enough times I was certain I had figured it out. Before I knew what happened, I was engaged in some friendly wagering and after losing several attempts at a free soda the stakes began to grow. The gentleman finally promised me one more chance but warned me that should I lose I would be enslaved to mow his lawn. At that point in my life there could not have been a worse fate than having to mow my own lawn, much less anyone else's." But that didn't keep Minter from trying one more time. But once again, Preacher's hand was quicker than the eye. Minter remembers the man feeling sorry for him and offering the hope of a double-or-nothing chance to get out of his horrific debt. And of course, he lost again.

Fast forward to Minter's wedding day in October 1988. "I remember standing in the hall with Rev. Freeland and my dad, nervous and waiting to make my entrance [into the sanctuary]. Reverend Freeland eased my obvious anxiety by reminding me that getting married did not excuse my unpaid grass cutting debt and that it had grown extremely high over all those years."

Minter and his wife, Julie, later had two boys, Steven and Matthew. The couple served in the Portsmouth Alliance Church for many years, and both their sons had the privilege early in their lives of interacting with Preacher and getting to know a true man of God. Steve, who thanked God they got that chance, always wondered, though, which one of his boys would be the first to fall for the hidden quarter trick.

Elbert and June Crawford came to know Preacher in 1975 when they started attending Portsmouth Alliance. They both fondly remembered a remark he made on a visit in their home. He told them, "If you are looking for a perfect church we are not it, because I'm a part of it." June Crawford also remembered the Sunday night the Freelands invited Eugene and Beverly McNeal and she and her husband, Elbert, over to the parsonage for refreshments after church. "Reverend Freeland had a habit of calling me Jean instead of June, so this particular Sunday night he called on 'Gene' to say the blessing and who do you suppose said it — me. Coming home I thought it strange that he would call on me to pray when there were men at the table. I soon learned he had meant Gene McNeal and not me. Later on we all had a good laugh."

As summer approached it was time for the 1974-75 class of the Alliance Christian School to graduate — all 14 of them. A few weeks later, Preacher was preparing his Sunday sermon when he remembered once reading an article in the New York Times about a little boy named Billy Maher who, in chalk on the wall of the New York City Public Library, had drawn a heart and written "B.M. loves everybody" in the middle of it. Preacher wondered what had become of Billy. He wondered if his feelings were still the same or if the world and its cares had gotten in the way. Reading in the second chapter of Revelation he came across a verse and knew exactly what God wanted him to share with church family:

"Yet I hold this against you; You have forsaken your first love." **Revelation 2:4 (NIV)**

Choosing the title "What Ever Happened to Billy Maher?" Preacher spoke of the fact that many of us start off like Billy and then the world knocks the daylights out of us. We loved to go to church but other events in our lives interfere. We loved to pray but now our children seldom if ever see us kneel in prayer. We loved everybody only to learn they had let us down. Pausing for a moment, Preacher then looked over the sanctuary and asked the question, "What has happened to you?" He then challenged the crowd to pick up the chalk of life and write in bold print, "I love everybody — I love Jesus, His work, His people, His house, Him." Several men and women marched to the altar and accepted the Lord when the invitation was given.

As a grand climax to 1975, Rev. Freeland was invited to preach a Christmas message to the thousands who listened to WXRI, a popular local radio station. Choosing **Matthew 1:18-24** as his scripture, he told "The Story of Christmas" and how Jesus had come to earth as a baby to save a lost world.

Early the next year, Preacher finally received some much needed help. The church was averaging just over 300 people in Sunday School each week and nearly 350 for the morning service. Preacher was preparing three sermons a week, handling just about all of the church's administrative duties, working daily at the school, and... well, steering the ship while doing most of the rowing, too. In February, Glenn Lewis arrived to serve as the assistant pastor. He was a 1973 graduate of Nyack College and was now working on his masters degree. Lewis was well-loved from the day he arrived, and like Preacher, had a special knack relating to kids and teenagers. After several very busy years, he and his family left Portsmouth for the missions field in Thailand. After that, Lewis and his wife, Shelia, served many years as dorm parents at the Back Forest Academy in Germany — an English-speaking Christian school for missionary kids.

In March 1976, Alliance also hired its first paid secretary. Marcia Stacey, a 1975 graduate of Toccoa Falls College, held the position until the summer of 1978 when she left to become the denomination's South Atlantic District secretary.

The summer of 1976 included a surprise phone call from Preacher's old friend Austin Peterson, who had been instrumental in building the parsonage in Union City, PA, and who had drawn up the blueprints for the new church in Portsmouth. Peterson was now an area supervisor for the Alaskan pipeline in Purdah Bay and was calling to invite Preacher to come for three weeks and preach to the 2,000 or so men who worked there. After receiving the unanimous blessing of his church family, Preacher accepted the invitation and started making preparations for the early October trip. Reverend H.L. Talbot, a retired minister who had pastored nearby Alexander Baptist for many years, agreed to fill the pulpit while Preacher was gone.

In discussing the trip with Peterson, several things became obvious. First, Preacher would need to bring plenty of sermon material. The schedule included preaching nightly and twice on Sunday for three weeks. Second, Peterson casually mentioned it would be 30 degree below zero by the time the missions trip was over. Preacher would need to bring all the long Johns he could find. And third, according to Peterson, the only semblance of a religious service currently was an informal prayer meeting on Thursday nights that attracted about a dozen men. Preacher would need to bring his power of persuasion to help get people to come. On a bright note, Peterson did tell him that the services were to be held in a newly-finished theater equipped with an organ and piano.

When Preacher returned home from Alaska, he was interviewed by a staff reporter for the *Virginian-Pilot* newspaper. The article written by Chris Gwyn expertly described and poignantly captured the hard work (14-16 hours a day, seven days a week) and sense of isolation (200 miles within the Arctic Circle) the pipeline workers faced each day. It also mentioned how handsomely they were paid (nearly $2,000 per week). Still, Preacher somehow turned what was primarily intended to be a human interest story into a testimony for the ministry of Christ. Included in the article were these quotes from him: "God works in mysterious ways, His wonders to perform. Some of these men had to come from a lush civilization to a forsaken wilderness to find their God and Savior... A number of the men told me that when they get back home they are going to work in the church... All of the men don't go on the pipeline for the money. There is a small nucleus who went down there to witness for the Lord."

Once back, Preacher was elated to find there were now 148 students enrolled in the school — a real breakthrough. He couldn't help but marvel at God's endless goodness. Still, he did have one concern. It felt really, really warm in his office. He'd need to get that thermostat checked again.

Chapter 28

35 Years Old And Still Going Strong

"Great is the Lord and most worthy of praise, His greatness no one can even fathom. One generation will commend your works to another, they will tell of your mighty acts." **Psalm 145:3-4 (NIV)**

January 1, 1977, shivered in on the coattails of a cold winter. But Preacher was ready for it. The three-week mission trip to Alaska a few months before had taught him to dress warmly — or frozen his senses, completely — and the friendly people in the church could turn the worst blizzard into one filled with the warm glow of the love of God, anyhow. He prayed daily for the leadership of Portsmouth Alliance and was especially grateful the Lord had sent those with special talents to be part of the church family — especially those who were gifted in music. If there were any doubts who had the best Gospel music program in the area one need only visit Alliance on a Sunday morning or night. If Chuck Conti or Delores Taylor didn't bless with a solo, one of the other soloists, duets or trios certainly would.

In early February, while seeking the Lord's will for the Sunday message, Preacher's thoughts turned to all that enormous talent. And then he was checked by the Holy Spirit. The church was filled with 350 or so worshippers each Sunday morning. He wondered if each of them realized they had a gift God wanted them to use for His glory. After all, he realized, the Bible clearly stated it took many different talents to make a body of believers. He wanted to make sure each individual knew that. While in prayer, he was led to the parable of the talents found in the Gospel of Matthew:

"Then the one man who had received the one talent came. Master, he said, I knew that you are a hard man, harvesting where you have not sown and gathering where you have not scattered seed. So I was afraid and went out and hid your talent in the ground. See, here is what belongs to you." **Matthew 25:24-25 (NIV)**

Preacher spoke from his heart that Sunday morning. "Maybe you have but one small talent. So what? Use it. Go to the Lord in prayer and ask Him to help you discover and use your talent. You might be surprised. Whatever you do, don't bury your talent. The church needs it."

Preacher was never far from the school and would walk the halls almost daily, spreading cheer and words of encouragement. It was his desire that every teacher and student felt like a part of the Alliance family. During the year, the mother of Caroline Pond, the young phys ed teacher, became very ill and was in the hospital for about two months. Preacher and Freda took her into their home and treated her like their adopted daughter. One morning Freda went to work at the school and left Preacher in charge of fixing breakfast for Pond and himself. The eggs turned out fine — maybe a little runny, he remembered — but something had gone terribly wrong with the pancakes, leaving them uncooked in the middle. When Freda returned home and found the pancakes in the trash she declared Preacher's cooking days to be over. Preacher visited often with Pond's mother before her death in 1978 and continued to "watch over" her girl.

Another milestone was about to take place. The Portsmouth Alliance Church would be celebrating its 35th anniversary and an entire week of events was planned for June 19-26. As part of the celebration, a commemorative program was put together which included the following greeting penned by Preacher:

— — —

Dear Friends,

"Great is the Lord and greatly to be praised, and His greatness is unsearchable. One generation shall laud Thy works to another, and shall declare Thy mighty acts." Psalm 145:3-4

Thirty-five years. Thirty-five years of proclaiming the wondrous Gospel of Christ. Out of the acorn the oak has grown. Men and women and young people who love God have watered the seed with tears and God has given the increase.

To condense thirty-five years of exciting answer to prayer on a page is impossible. Thousands of dollars have gone to support missions around the world. Hundreds of service men have been saved through the ministry of this church and today are scattered all over the world, many doing their part to further the Gospel. Many others have found Christ here and have moved to other parts of America. It would take two churches this size to accommodate all who have passed through our doors.

The church today continues to reach out in many directions: a daily radio broadcast; our Christian high school; Stockade boys and Pioneer girls; weekly visitation; Sunday School and individual Christians witnessing to God's goodness. Surely God has blessed us.

Thirty-five years. Will God grant us another thirty-five? As we view the signs of His coming our heart cry becomes, "Help us Lord to continue the task which You have called us."

Your Pastor, Rev. Earl Freeland

— — —

The program also included a special tribute to Virginia Holland Cuthriell, who had attended the church since its inception, and a list of congregation members who through the years had gone on to become pastors, pastor's wives, and assistant pastors.

Realizing the week and its events would eventually fade away, Preacher saved a copy of the program and filed it with what was now a large number of sermon outlines, notes, illustrations and other unidentifiable pieces of paper he had collected through the years. And for a moment his thoughts turned backward. He was now 61 — 30 years as a Christian & Missionary Alliance pastor, 18 of which had been spent in Portsmouth. He wandered what God had in store for him and the family of the Portsmouth Alliance Church.

Chapter 29

The 'Singingest' Church You Ever Heard

"Sing to the Lord you Saints of His, praise His Holy name." **Psalm 30:4 (NIV)**

Sports stole many of the headlines at Alliance Christian during the 1977-78 school year. Now with 168 students, it was easy to field teams and even start a few new ones. Preacher attended so many contests that he sometimes found himself wondering how he would fit in all of his "regular" duties at the church. But he'd always be in the stands or standing on the sidelines, cheering on his "kids."

The school fielded its first boy's soccer team and finished second in the conference. When basketball season rolled around, there were so many boys at tryouts that a junior varsity team was formed. Needing coaches, Preacher brought in outside help by asking church members Linwood Minter and Bobby Hoffman to oversee the basketball program. Minter had fond memories of his nights on the sideline. "The Rev as we affectionately called him approached Bobby Hoffman and me to ask if we would consider coaching the basketball team. Although Bobby and I had full-time jobs the opportunity for me to realize one of my fantasies, coaching, was certainly to my liking. The opportunity to work with young men in a Christian setting was an experience I will always cherish. Later, when I was appointed to the school board and became the chairman I was able to hire one of the young men I had coached to become the school athletic director." Attention in the spring turned to boy's baseball and girl's softball with both teams winning conference championships.

Swished jump shots and blasted home runs weren't the only exciting things happening at the Alliance complex. On May 6, 1978, Portsmouth Mayor, Jack Barnes, was once again officiating as ground was broken for a new library and four new classrooms. With Preacher and many others looking on, the school chorus sang *"We've Come This Far By Faith."* Boy, had they ever. A few weeks later 23 seniors walked across the stage to receive their diplomas and Preacher felt as proud as he had when his own children had graduated. After all, he thought of each of them as his own.

One of those graduates was Tammy Shaw, who would later become a teacher at Alliance. The next year Preacher married Ben Cross, a 1976 graduate of Alliance, and Tammy. A few years later the couple would seek Preacher's love and guidance. Tammy remembered that night. "In April 1982 we found out that Ben's dad had lung cancer and Ben, who was still not a Christian, needed to talk to someone he trusted and someone he knew would have the answers. Ben and I went to Rev. Freeland's house late one night after visiting Ben's dad in the hospital. Reverend

Freeland saw Ben's need. The three of us knelt in his living room that night as Ben asked Christ to be his personal Savior."

It was also a banner year for the Portsmouth Alliance Church, and especially, the music program. Soloists were plentiful; Chuck Conti, Billy Barker, Delores Taylor and a host of others. Groups included the Alliance Trio and the Family Tree-O. During 1978 the Family Tree-O, consisting of Louise Beale, Trish Aydlett and Polly Wand — with Belinda Beale playing the piano — produced their first record, "In Everything Give Thanks." The album took on mythical proportions over the years much like a Christmas fruitcake. While produced in limited quantity, it seemed everybody who attended Alliance past, present and future owned a copy of it. And then there was the Alliance choir. No one in the Tidewater area questioned it was the best this side of Heaven. But what most people didn't know was that they were very observant. Since the choir set in the loft right behind Preacher on stage, members saw and heard things no one else did. Wanting to share this behind-the-scenes experience with others, Imogene Bland wrote a poem entitled "How the Choir Sees the Preacher" which was read to the congregation on April 6, 1978. It deserves a second look:

— — —

>We often think of preachers
>As a breed that's set apart.
>And often we're inclined to think
>They're not human as we are.
>But they are, they really are
>If you don't believe it just ask the choir.
>
>At his back we're asked to sit
>He sings along — we shout.
>He thinks he's giving us his best
>We try to drown him out.
>He sings off key and just a bit sour
>If you don't believe it just ask the choir.
>
>Bad days he's had a time or two
>I'm sure that that's not news.
>But from the back we plainly saw
>He had on two different color shoes.
>We laughed so hard tears came in showers
>If you don't believe it just ask the choir.
>
>He sometimes has new clothes to sport
>He calls his old ones "rags."
>And in his great excitement

He forgets to clip the tags.

How oft' you've seen him pound the desk
It seems it almost smokes.
But from behind we see the same
'cept it scattered all his notes.
That's when our faces show a glower
If you don't believe it just ask the choir.

You only saw him from the front
All spruced and scrubbed and shorn.
But from the back the view was changed
We saw his pants were torn.
Yes, they were, they truly were
If you don't believe it, just ask the choir.

We've had our fun with Preacher
And every word is true.
We can say these things about him
But we sure do dare you to.
Cause we love him and he's all ours
If you don't believe it, just ask the choir.

— — —

August 28 that year was another special day for Preacher as he married two members of the Alliance Christian High School graduating class of 1975 — Tim Lane and Margaret Keeter. Lane remembered some advice Preacher gave them. "Always leave a little time for each other. Even after you have children, go somewhere once a week and eat an ice cream cone and just talk." Preacher had given similar advice many times in the past and would do so many times in the future.

Also during that summer Preacher's secretary, Marcia Stacey, broke it to him that she had been offered the job as district secretary for the South Atlantic District of the Christian & Missionary Church and felt it was the Lord's will. Hearing Preacher would be needing a new secretary, Judy Jackson mentioned to him her interest in the job. She and her husband, Denny, had moved to Norfolk from Washington, DC, about a year before when her husband's company transferred him. Since Judy had attended St. Paul Bible College (an Alliance college), they had chosen to worship at the Portsmouth Alliance Church. With two small children, Judy had chosen not to work when they first arrived in the area but felt strongly it was the Lord's will that she use her skills for His glory. By now they had moved to Portsmouth to be nearer the church and she believed "keeping Preacher straight" was her calling. After not hearing anything for a couple of months, Preacher approached Jackson in early October and asked her if she could come to work the next Monday — just like that. He then asked her if three dollars an hour was good but she was able to negotiate a whole extra quarter. When she arrived at work the next week, Preacher showed Jackson her office which was filled with everything form paint brushes to cleaning supplies. After spending the entire day cleaning out the room she finally found the desk and an old beat-up typewriter. Jackson immediately became his "right hand man" and proved invaluable both to Preacher and the pastors who followed.

Preacher and Jackson has a great working relationship from the first day. "Realizing I had two small children at home he made by job easier by allowing me to leave and take care of them if needed. After I learned the trick to getting the typewriter to work I was set to go. My hours were nine to two and Preacher was always there when I arrived, usually feeding the birds. He spent most mornings studying and afternoons visiting members and those in the hospital. He was never too busy to help someone out, often putting on work clothes to spend time helping a member build or repair something."

Jackson also had a front row seat when it came to Preacher's mischievous side. She fondly remembered the relationship he had with Chuck Conti. "Preacher loved to do things with Chuck. It wasn't unusual for him, in the middle of a sermon, to turn and say to Chuck, 'Chuck, I feel like singing, let's sing.' The church family loved those times. There were also the fun times. Like the morning Chuck wandered into the office with a container of orange juice in hand. Sitting the juice on the corner of Preacher's desk Chuck went somewhere for a few minutes. Preacher couldn't let the opportunity pass, so he made a small hole in the side of the container and drained most of the orange juice out. After sealing it back up he filled it with water. Chuck returned and started drinking his orange juice, not saying a word but looking kind of funny. Preacher finally confessed that 'somebody' might have messed with it."

By 1979 Portsmouth Alliance was averaging 381 people for Sunday morning services. Special occasions like Easter drew over 600 worshippers, requiring the deacons and ushers to open the two overflow rooms near the front of the sanctuary. And to the delight of Preacher, some of the musicians in his church were spreading their wings. With the release of the album *"I Saw A Man,"* Conti made his debut as a Gospel recording artist. Rich with old-time favorites the album featured the songs *"Down From His Glory," "How Great Thou Are," "Because He Lives"* and *"Til the Storm Passes On."* A few months later Delores Taylor released a solo album entitled *"Closer to Home"* which included great songs of faith such as *"Jesus Came and Touched Me," "There's a Place at the Cross"* and *"Streets of Gold."* And after much urging from church members, the Alliance Trio of Taylor, Pat Hutchens and Kathy Branch recorded *"The Sounds Of His Coming"* which featured such classics as *"God's Family," "Falling in Love With Him"* and *"Jesus is the Answer."* Those of us fortunate to still have these albums — and something to play them on — continue to be blessed even today.

With all the great singing going on, Preacher still managed to get in a sermon or two. One in particular had a big impact on the congregation. It was entitled "Weighed and Found Wanting" with scripture taken from the fifth chapter of Daniel:

"This is what these words mean. Mene: God has numbered the days of your reign and brought it to an end. Tekel: You have been weighed on the scales and found wanting." **Daniel 5:26-27 (NIV)**

Preacher encouraged his flock to turn their loves over to Him who can make you a new person. Then, when you step on the scales of life, you will find love, kindness, compassion, obedience, prayer, giving and service.

Chapter 30

Instruments Of God

"For to me, to live is Christ and to die is gain." **Philippians 1:21 (NIV)**

Preacher used years 1980-86 to ensure his Father's house in Portsmouth, VA, was in order and on solid ground. As the decade commenced, he rejoiced in all God had done for Alliance. The Sunday morning crowds at the church were fast approaching 400 and the Sunday School attendance already exceeded 300. The school was meeting the needs of the city and surrounding areas and would probably be expanded to include kindergarten through grade school the next fall. At age 61 he had given no serious thought of retirement. But, in the back of Preacher's mind, he knew sooner than later his ministry as pastor of Portsmouth Alliance would end and he wanted to be sure the church was in good shape both spiritually and financially. He felt the same way about the school which he dearly loved. Already he had come to rely more and more on Judy Jackson, his secretary. He thanked the Lord for her daily and knew when the time came for him to step down she would bear a heavy responsibility to provide continuity to the ministry. And though he was as active as ever, Jackson, too, sensed Preacher's "nesting" spirit. "The years I spent with Preacher were special. He was more than a boss, he was a friend. He loved the church and the school, especially the young people. You could clearly see his love as Preacher hugged on the children at school. Preacher Freeland had a real burden to see people come to know the Lord, which was the real reason he started the school. He modeled what a preacher should be — Christ like."

It seemed to Preacher no sooner had the last senior walked across the stage that is was time to start hiring teachers for the 1980-81 school year. Only this time, they'd be interviewing not only for high school positions but kindergarten and grade school, as well. With the expansion came a new name, Alliance Christian School. The hiring process had just gotten started when God sent the perfect kindergarten teacher, Inez Fletcher. For the next 15 years she would be the start of formal education for hundreds of young boys and girls. "I remember how excited Rev. Freeland was the year the school started kindergarten classes. At least once a week he would stop by our classroom to see what we were doing and ask the students if they would say their Bible verses for him. Then he would praise them and tell them what a great job they were doing. Sometimes he would stop by just to bring the children a treat." Fletcher retired in 1995, replaced but never to be forgotten.

Although the school went that year without a head administrator, Tom Ballance — who was the assistant administrator the year before and taught Bible and history — filled in admirably. Nineteen seniors received their diplomas in early June 1981. Among those graduating was Ann Robertson, daughter of television evangelist and Christian Broadcasting Network (CBN) founder Pat Robertson.

God continued to bless the Portsmouth Alliance Church, as well. As attendance continued to grow so did the different ministries of the church. Preacher was thankful for the many leaders God had sent their way. Unlike the "old days" he was not expected to attend to every detail. This suited him fine and allowed more time for sermon preparation. And spending more time with his flock. Although 400 or more people attended the Sunday morning service each week. Preacher made it a point to know — or get to know — each one of them personally. With a congregation that large, he knew some had never made a commitment to Jesus Christ and many others had needs and burdens too heavy for them to bear. With this in mind, on a Sunday morning in early 1981, he preached a sermon entitled "Oh That I Might Find Him" from Job:

"Then Job replied. Even today my complaint is bitter; his hand is heavy in spite of my groaning. If only I knew where to find him; if only I could go to his dwelling." **Job 23:1-3 (NIV)**

During the sermon Preacher asked several "are you" questions and provided the answers. Are you sick? He is the great physician. Are you perplexed? He is the great problem solver. Are you in need of peace? He is the great comforter. Are you in need of pardon? He is the great forgiver. Several people had accepted Christ as their Savior when he had preached the same sermon to the Portsmouth church in 1961. Although no one responded to the altar call this time, another seed had been planted.

The first sign of spring weather found Preacher on the golf course whenever he could manage it. Linwood Minter found himself partnered with the "Rev" on one of those days. "My good friend Bobby Hoffman invited Lee Smith, Preacher, and me to join him in a round of golf. Although Preacher and I loved to play it was a good day if we broke 100. Bobby and Lee were excellent golfers and quite capable of shooting in the low 80s. You can imagine my astonishment when Preacher challenged them to a round based on total strokes with no handicap. When I questioned his sanity he assured me it was all right since we were only playing for cokes and hot dogs. Although we all figured something was up, Bobby and Lee agreed. After nine holes Preacher had shot a 51 and I had posted a 46. As we took a deep breath before heading to the tenth tee, I commented to Preacher that although we were playing pretty good golf we were 21 strokes behind and in deep trouble. With a grin I had seen so often he told me there was no problem since he was through for the day and if I could shoot a 50 on the back nine Bobby and Lee didn't have a chance. When I told Bobby and Lee that Preacher was through counting his strokes and was on his way home, they were laughing so hard we probably could have won anyway."

If Portsmouth Alliance had printed its own newspaper, two headlines in particular would have stood out in the second half of 1981. The first banner would have read, "Another Banner Year for the School Begins." With Michael Ellis as the new administrator, Alliance Christian School opened the 1981-82 year with 245 students in grades kindergarten through 12. "Alliance Trio Sings at the White House" would have been the second headline to jump off the page. Singing in President's Park South (commonly called the Ellipse located just south of the White House fence) with a proud Preacher and other church members cheering them on, the trio gave a beautiful concert which became the album *"Withholding Nothing"* featuring such songs as *"Praise You," "Emmanuel," "I Have a Friend"* and *"Worth Calvary."*

Under the leadership of new principal Michael Ellis, Alliance Christian School enjoyed a tremendous year. The athletic program continued to pile up Metro Conference championships. More importantly, the school made great strides in academic excellence. Most of the 24 seniors would be attending college in the fall. At the 1982 graduation ceremony, Preacher prayed that each one of them would become sound Christians and spread the truths about Christ they had been taught in school to their entire sphere of influence.

Likewise, the Portsmouth Alliance Church continued to prosper with new people visiting on Sundays. Some came to hear the great music; others to hear what God had to say to them through the inspired sermons of Preacher. Most of them liked what they heard and became members. If Preacher had slowed down a bit it wasn't noticeable as he filled the pulpit twice on Sundays and again on Wednesday nights. The rest of his week was spent sharing the love of Christ with all he came in contact with. One place he visited on a weekly basis was the insurance company owned by Charlie Mason. Mason's wife, Frances, cherished those times. "He would come by our insurance company every week and have prayer with us. I remember that on one occasion while he was praying a man from North Carolina was in the other room taking care of his insurance and listening. He later called to let us know that while listening to Preacher he accepted the Lord as his personal Savior."

To Preacher, being a pastor was a 24-hour-a-day calling. One afternoon, while being interviewed for this book, he gave his "job" description: "I tried to be present at every athletic or special event the school or church had. I felt I should be there and it helped that I love sports and people. I wanted the kids to know I was interested in them as a person. That is critical. I would like say again that when you are a pastor it has to be a total ministry. Every minute and everywhere you are you represent the Lord as one of his called ministers. I told my son-in-law, who is an Alliance pastor, that every time you step out of your house you are representing the Lord and your church family. How you look and how you act. That is one of my philosophies. I represent the King. Of course I would rather sometimes wear jeans and a sports shirt but even now as a retired minister I try to represent Him well."

One of those who fondly remembered 1982 as the year she came to know and love

Preacher was Priscilla Key, my wife. "Preacher Earl Freeland entered my life when Bud, Buddy and I started visiting the Portsmouth Alliance Church and later became members. We were members of another church and passed by Alliance each Sunday. At first we would attend occasionally for the evening service to hear the great music. We soon found the music merely complimented the great preaching we heard. From the beginning I not only found a true pastor but a true friend."

My wife often good-naturally referred to Preacher as trouble with a capital "T." He always had the knack of saying or doing something witty and mischievous. And you could never get anything past him. Take for instance my first pair of non-wrinkle chino slacks. Here's how she remembers it: "Bud and Preacher were at the baseball field behind the school, where they usually were, cleaning up some tree branches and other trash around the bleachers. Preacher wanted something from his garage and commissioned Bud to get it. As a short cut Bud decided to jump over a three-foot wire fence separating the field from the parsonage. Somehow Bud got tangled up in that wire and tore the whole knee out of those beautiful new slacks. When he got home he explained in great detail how it was all Preacher's fault, so the following Sunday I confronted him in front of God and a good portion of the church family. Without a second's hesitation Preacher informed me there was no problem. I could just cut them off and Bud would have instant Bermuda shorts. Now you tell me how I could respond to that inspired reasoning?

As if that wasn't bad enough a few weeks later Bud came home and informed me that he and Preacher were lucky they weren't spending the next few days in jail. It seems Philbrick Plumbing Company had donated an old truck to the school. Not knowing the truck transmission was shot and was waiting to be repaired, they loaded it with all kids of rubble to transport to the road for trash pick up. Bud jumped into the driver's seat with his faithful partner beside him, started the truck and then tried to find a gear that would cause it to move. Amid some awful grinding and scraping, Bud and Preacher saw and heard the school maintenance man running across the field yelling and shouting at the top of his voice. He didn't care if was the church pastor, nobody was going to drive his 'new' truck. Bud said he worked some scary investigations when he was with the Naval Investigative Service (NIS) but nothing quite like that."

My wife will always hold a very special place in her heart for Preacher. "Preacher Freeland was with our family from the very beginning, participating in my son Buddy and Crystal's wedding, dedicating our grandchildren, through my mother's introduction to the Christian & Missionary Alliance Church, her illness and death from cancer, Bud's serious accident and all the special times shared in fellowship and long talks. Truly he was a man's man but was also a fellow Christian's support."

How precious were the years from 1982-86. To use a baseball analogy, Preacher had reached third base and was heading for the home plate of his active ministry as pastor of the Portsmouth Alliance Church. Although he didn't think of it in those terms he used each sermon to prepare his church family for a richer Christian experience. Again, he wanted to make sure his church family was prepared for the day when he would step down as their pastor. There were so many great and encouraging messages during those last few years. A search through the files of a battered old metal filing cabinet (and various shapes and sizes of brief cases) in Preacher's study after his retirement was like discovering manna from heaven. Among the many notes and illustrations found was the entire text of a message he preached Sept. 30, 1984, at the age of 68. The message is a fitting tribute to a man who never wanted to be anything more than an instrument used by God. It is a sermon I believe the Lord wants readers of this book to hear:

— — —

"Instruments of God"
Message by Rev. Earl Freeland
30 September 1984 — 11:00 A.M.
Portsmouth, Virginia
Portsmouth Alliance Church

"According to my earnest expectation and my hope that in nothing I shall be ashamed, but that with all boldness, as always, so now also Christ shall be magnified in by body, whether it be by life, or death. For me to live is Christ, and to die is gain." **Philippians 1:20-21**

"My friends, I have no doubt in my own mind that you always are quite full of goodness and equipped with knowledge of every kind, well able to give advice to one another. Nevertheless I have written to refresh your memory and written somewhat boldly at times in virtue of the gift I have from God. His grace has made me a minister of Christ Jesus to the Gentiles. My priestly service is the preaching of the gospel of Christ and it falls to me to offer the Gentiles to Him as an acceptable sacrifice, consecrated by the Holy Spirit. Thus in the fellowship of Christ I have grounds for pride in the service. I will venture to speak of those things alone in which I have been Christ's instrument to bring the Gentiles into allegiance by word and deed by the force of miraculous signs and by the power of the Holy Spirit." **Romans 15:14-19**

Paul is speaking to the Philippians, speaking to a young, 10-year-old church, and in the book of Romans he is reiterating what he had written to these Christians; that he was dedicating himself completely to the Master. While writing to the Romans, Paul was in Corinth. I see him pacing the floor, as he thinks, as he prays, writes and dictates this tremendous book of Romans to his secretary. He's opening his heart to them in saying, "I would like to come to you but in lieu of the fact that I cannot come to you personally I'm going to write this letter of Romans."
If you will check you will find that the church in Rome was in the middle of the

teeming capital of the world. Hoards of people were there. Paul was writing to them in this great, classic book, probing great theological issues and giving them God's great plan of salvation. Too, he is describing human nature and the work of the Holy Spirit along with his own frustrations and the battle with the enemy to keep him from being what he really wanted to be for God. So we find in this 15th chapter Paul comes to the end of a great benediction. "And may the God of hope fill you with joy and peace by faith in Him, until the power of the Holy Spirit make you overflow with hope"... You overflow with hope.

Do you catch the symbolism? That you might be so full that you overflow, and not a surface kind of experience. It's an experience that fills until it bubbles out like an artesian well. When Paul comes to the end of that great benediction, it seems the book should close. Instead he catches his breath and adds a personal word of testimony. "I will venture to speak these things alone in which I have been." This is the thrust of my message to you this morning, "in which I have been Christ's instrument to bring the Gentiles to Him as an offering."

What a picture... he didn't say "that I might be an instrument"... he said, I am that instrument. He did not say I'm a great preacher. I'm a great theologian. I'm a great missionary. I'm a great writer. I do this or I do that. That was the farthest thing from his mind. He said I want you to know "I am an instrument." Now think with me this morning. An instrument links one thing to another. Let me illustrate it this way. On my vacation this year I was fishing in a little private pond for rainbow trout. Becoming thirsty we walked up the side of the mountain where we found someone had driven a pipe into a little crevice in the rock. Flowing through that pipe was crystal clear water so cold it hurt your teeth when you drank it. We drank and drank. I cupped my hands and that pipe became the instrument that brought beautiful cold water to my thirsty lips. It was an instrument standing between me and that refreshing water. A link.

You see, an instrument conveys something. The organ conveys a message. The piano conveys a message. The choir becomes an instrument to convey a message. The soloist becomes an instrument conveying a message. Wherever we are, Paul said, "I am an instrument." He illustrated in the book of Corinthians by saying, "I am an ambassador." I'm one sent with a vital message of life or death. So he is saying here, I want to be the conductor of a life or death message to a lost and undone world. I want to be that instrument. But he doesn't stop there. He goes on to say back in verse 14, "I have no doubt in my own mind that you yourselves are quite full of goodness and equipped with knowledge of every kind, and will be able to give advice to another."

So what's Paul saying? He's saying that whatever I am, you are capable of being. There is no difference between us. God is looking for willing individuals to convey a message to the lost world. God is looking for an instrument through which He can supply that need. Paul is not looking for prima donnas, those who were interested in serving only because they would be seen or heard or patted on the back. He was looking for those who would say, "Holy Spirit, use me as an instrument." And listen; the Holy Spirit is looking for tools... instruments through which He can operate.

When He finds a man or woman willing to dedicate themselves to that end He uses them. You see, a carpenter picks up a hammer and uses that instrument, or a saw. Our brother picks up a trumpet and uses that instrument to convey a message. Think with me for a moment. Here's a giant orchestra. The potential is there for beautiful music. The conductor is leading. All of a sudden he calls for the violins to begin to play — it's their art — but not one sound. He looks. The violinists are not there, leaving a blank space in the music. He goes on and after a while calls for the trombones — silence — the trombone section is empty. There are no instruments to be used. The rest of the orchestra has lost its power because there's a void in these sections.

Now what I want you to see is simply this. God sees blank spaces when He wants to orchestrate His message to a lost and dying world. He says here's a need and here's a way to meet that need. He asks in the Old Testament, "Who will stand in the gap. Who will be an instrument of God."

You remember what Jesus prayed — "That they may all be one, as Thou Father are in me and I in Thee, that they also may be in us so that the world may believe Thou hast sent me."

My dear friend, in one sense it matters very little what you believe. You may believe that the Holy Spirit is real. You may believe in the trinity. You may believe in the word of God. You believe right down the line and say I believe... I believe... I believe. But let me tell you, unless there has been a definite experience in your life where you personally met Jesus Christ as your Savior, you may believe yourself right into hell.

In chapter 13 Paul said, "God will fill you with joy and peace by your faith in Him." Now, to whom is Paul speaking? He's speaking to special people. He's speaking to people he hoped would be sold out, so he could convey to them the need that God had for instruments and would stand up to say, "I will be that instrument." Let me share with you. Go into any doctor's office and you find that instruments to be used have been thoroughly cleansed.

May I open my heart to you this morning? More and more I am concerned that Christians are becoming like the world instead of like Jesus Christ. Let me explain what I mean. I'm concerned when Christians feel they can have a glass of wine with a meal; or smoke a joint; or that little off-colored joke won't amount to too much; or that an affair on the side isn't too far out of line. My God Christians. God can never use you as an instrument. God does not fill garbage cans. He fills those who are cleansed instruments. "That you might be filled," He said, "with the Holy Spirit."

There are those who see no harm in anything any more and feel they can disobey God outright without retribution. Not so. God does not work like that. God is not blind. I heard someone say, "Some people live like they think God's blind." But He isn't. He wants vessels that are clean — instruments who will obey the will of God. You see, no man can ask God to bless him if he's planning on robbing a bank. No woman can ask God to bless her if she's going to live in adultery. That's what I'm trying to get across to you.

I will never forget. In my first church in Union City, Pennsylvania, I had a mail man whose name was Hoggie, believe it or not, and he would stop and talk to me almost every day. For the first few weeks I was just getting acquainted with him and he always had a big chew of tobacco in his mouth. I thought, man, if someone ever hit him on the back and he swallowed that chew he'd choke to death. Two or three weeks after we got acquainted Hoggie told me he was a Christian and started quoting me scripture. Young and foolish at the time I said to him, "Hoggie, do you think you can squirt tobacco juice out of one side of your mouth and scripture out of the other and God's going to bless it." I might as well have hit him in the head with a ball bat. He turned a little white for a minute or two and turned and walked away.

About a week later he came back to deliver my mail again and said to me, "Preacher, no one ever checked me on that before and I want to thank you. You notice I don't have the chew this morning." My dear friend, God's looking for clean vessels He can use as instruments for His honor and glory. You see, water is either bitter or sweet. It can't be salty and fresh at the same time. That's what the scripture said, isn't it?

Now look with me again at verse 18 and there you will find he is saying, "God has used me as an instrument by word and by deed." Not just by word alone but by deed as well. He wanted these people to realize they were not playing games. Colossians said this, "Whatsoever you do in word or deed, do everything in the name of the Lord Jesus Christ." First John lists this powerful call in chapter 3 and verse 18 when he said, "Little children, let us not love in word or speech but in deed and in truth." Paul said, "I have been Christ's instrument by sign, by word and by deed."... By sign, by word, by deed.

Someone said, "How come we don't see miracles anymore like we did in the day of Paul." We do. In the day of Paul they didn't have the written word of God. God worked in an unusual way by miracles to prove Himself to be real. Although we now have the word of God we still have miracles. I tell you I've seen men come to Christ and whiskey turn into milk for the kids. I've seen men come to Christ and liars turn into truthful men; filthy into clean; lazy men become workers; drunk-

[139]

ards become sober; and useless men become useful men because the miracle of the new birth had taken place in their life. Thank God.

Now let me share one more thought with you. Look at verse 16 with me. "That I should be the minister of Jesus Christ to the Gentiles, ministering the gospel of God." When I came to this part of the scripture my heart almost jumped out of my shirt. Listen to what he was saying... "that the offering up of the Gentiles might be acceptable being sanctified by the Holy Ghost." What's he saying there? Ah, if you will just catch this with me. Paul was a Jewish man and he was thinking about Jewish terms and the Old Testament priesthood. Do you remember what the function of the Old Testament priesthood was? To take an offering in the very presence of God and the fire would come down and consume it as a symbol of being acceptable. Their job was to offer to God these sacrifices acceptable unto the Lord.

Now listen. Catch this picture. Paul said, "I am an instrument that I might bring the Gentiles to Christ, that I might offer them up as an offering to God as gratefulness for all he has done for me." What a picture! Lord! Here's my offering of love to you for all you've done for me.

When the Moravians first went to the West Indies to win men to Christ they were not able to get next to them because the owners of these slaves drove them with a whip to the fields at daylight and worked them until dark, leaving no opportunity to really share Christ with them. You know what those early missionaries did? They sold themselves as slaves to that master and when he drove them out into the field they worked side-by-side with these men and shared Jesus Christ with them. Ah, those men could say, "Lord here are these men from the West Indies. I offer them up as an offering to you." I ask you my dear family, what will your offering to the Master be?

You see, the thing that really is going to count is what God's done for you. That's true. Then, what God will do through you. "I'm an instrument Lord and I bring these Gentiles to you as an offering." Oh what a privilege to be a Sunday School teacher. Lord I bring these precious children to you that I've won in Christ as an offering. Young people's director — I bring these young people that I've won to you Lord as an offering. The choir using their voices as an offering to God. Sounds good but oftentimes the trouble with us? We're so selfish. We allow our lives to be cluttered with all kinds of things that keep the Spirit of God from operating through us to be the kind of instrument He would have us be. I close with a question. What will your offering be?

— — —

Chapter 31

Time To Step Down

"And he died for all, that those who live should no longer live for themselves but for him who died for them and was raised again. So from now on we regard no one from a worldly point of view. Though we once regarded Christ in this way, we do so no longer. Therefore, if anyone is in Christ, he is a new creation; the old has gone, the new has come." **II Corinthians 5:14-17 (NIV)**

We literally make millions of decisions in our lifetimes. A select few — like marriage, career choices, starting a family and, most importantly, where we will spend eternity — define who and what we become. In early 1987, Preacher found himself at one of those crossroads. With a great deal of sadness he realized it was about time to turn the reins of the Portsmouth Alliance Church over to a younger pastor. "Near the end I felt I wasn't as effective as I had been or should be. I felt more people should be accepting the Lord. I had a full-time assistant, Stephen Clark, who I had hoped would be the man to follow me but he left for another opportunity before I officially retired. I guess he got tired of waiting and figured I wasn't going to die anytime soon."

The numbers, however, suggested otherwise. From 1980 through the end of 1986, the average attendance on Sunday mornings had risen from 388 to 459 making Portsmouth Alliance one of the city's largest churches. In that same time span, the Alliance Christian School had grown from 270 students to 330. Still, Preacher prayed long and hard that God would send a man who would lead the church to even greater experiences in the Lord. Although he put off his decision for a while at the request of the church board, Preacher quietly retired on September 2, 1987, as pastor of the Portsmouth Christian & Missionary Alliance Church — a position he had held since June 1, 1959.

Upon his retirement, the governing board invited Preacher and Freda to remain in the parsonage the rest of their lives. He remained active and preached occasionally whenever Alliance was seeking a new pastor. And he often agreed to be the guest speaker at other churches. "There were many opportunities for me to preach in local churches and I did so. I had more time for my family and wood carving hobby, but I missed being a pastor. Bethany Baptist, down the street, invited me to be their intern pastor but I declined for two reasons. In my heart I was still the pastor of the Portsmouth Alliance Church and Bethany Baptist was too close. I didn't want any of the folks I pastored all those years at Portsmouth Alliance to follow me. I felt it would be more a hindrance to the Lord's work than any good it would do."

Instead, Preacher supported the pastors that followed him at Portsmouth Alliance, always willing to lend a helping hand but always being careful not to interfere with their ministry. As a retired pastor, he still held his credentials in the Christian & Missionary Alliance denomination and often participated in weddings, baby dedications and other functions. But again, always with the blessing of the current pastor. Preacher's interest and love for the Alliance Christian School never wavered, and even during sickness and injury, he managed his almost daily walk over just to say a kind word to a young student or teacher.

In fact, that love for the school was so great that in February 1988 he came out of retirement for a few months to serve as administrator. The school has seen three principals come and go since 1986 and the current one had resigned in the middle of the school year. *Virginian-Pilot* newspaper reporter, Ann Borrell, filed this story on Preacher's return:

— — —

When the Rev. Earl W. Freeland retired last year after 42 years in the Christian & Missionary Alliance Church ministry plans were under way for a trip this spring to the West Coast with his wife Freda. But in February those plans changed — as did the flagging morale at the Alliance Christian School — when Freeland was asked to take over as interim principal.

Though the twilight strolls and afternoons of sightseeing with his wife of fifty four years were delayed, Freeland, with others at the school he founded 18 years ago, believe it was the Holy Spirit's intervention that postponed that vacation as well as the minister's fleeting glimpse of retirement.

"Morale here was really low," says Nancy Zappulla, English teacher at the high school for four years. "We'd been without any formal leadership for over two months and before then the mood was restless." Health and personal reasons had led to the resignation of the previous two principals.

From church pulpit to school lectern Freeland's leadership is without question respected. He is described by students as one who has the rare ability to be a friend and disciplinarian. "He remembers specific things about each person," Zappulla says. "I guess you could say he makes people feel loved."

A walk down the hall with this warm hearted man brings clusters of students from kindergarten to 12th grade, offering handshakes, hugs and conversation. Like a proud father he notices their accomplishments, whether it's an athlete's performance or a student's artwork. "And it's not uncommon to see him mopping the floor or repairing a locker," Zappulla adds. "He leads by example."

"He's definitely made a difference here," says student body president Michael

Phillips. The 18 year old senior who has attended Alliance Christian School since eighth grade believes students quickly sense when a principal's concern is sincere. "And," he says, "Reverend Freeland really cares about us."

How does he do it? How does one of 73 years present an aura of agelessness and maintain a non-threatening close relationship with people of varying ages and backgrounds? "It has to be the Holy Spirit's presence," says the silver-haired preacher. "I give the Lord credit for the joy I feel inside and I try to pass that on to others."

Perhaps it is Freeland's availability to listen to and pray with students and the 30 staff members that makes him the source of inspiration they say he is. Rare is a visit with this congenial spirit that isn't filled with down to earth wit, conversation and hospitality. And for fifteen minutes each morning the teachers meet with him for devotions that they say are the best way to start the day.

"If we go to see him with a problem," third-grade teacher Joanna Hoornik says, "we never leave without a prayer said and steps made to a solution."

Freeland says he will miss the learning environment at the school when the year ends, knowing the school is searching for a permanent leader. But, as with most events in his life, he believes the Holy Spirit will lead the way. Questioned about his health he replied in his animated way: "Oh, I have the health of a mule. The Lord's seen to that too."

— — —

As if on cue, God did send a professional educator to Alliance — Dr. Claude Gates — who led the school until his retirement in 1995. Preacher knew he was the perfect hire. "I felt he [Dr. Gates] was God's man for the times. He brought professionalism to the position. The transition was smooth. He brought healing to the school. Too, he brought stability and credentials we needed for accreditation." After Dr. Gates' retirement, he wrote a letter of appreciation to Preacher and Freda:

Dear Rev. & Mrs. Freeland,

My purpose in writing to you is to tell you what you both meant to Dar and myself. Believe me, it is impossible to relate to you our total inward thoughts. But I will attempt to relate our thoughts in writing.

God made it possible for me to work with many pastors and educators. As a Pastor you are living proof that as you grow in years your wisdom as a gift from God increases. Your sermons we listened to gave us much to live by and encouragement. Each sermon got better. I am most appreciative the church did not put you out to pasture. Your messages to the students and staff were relevant and penetrating.

They always contained the truth from His Word. Of the pastors I have worked with you are one with whom I had the greatest respect. You were down to earth. As an educator God blessed you with vision that astounded me! How you started the school, how it grew and the light it was to the entire community is totally due to your faith and obedience to God as evident on the building, "To God Be The Glory." I consider it a great privilege to have had a small part in your vision. Your love for the students and the school was shown every day. I know your wife played an important part in the success of the school from the beginning till now. What a pleasure it was to have Mrs. Freeland attend a teacher appreciation dinner as honored guest and to see you present the final mortgage check to the bank. You were always there when I needed you. Thanks.

For His education,
Claude & Darlene Gates

— — —

Meanwhile, Rev. David Klinsing, who had come to the Portsmouth Alliance Church in 1991 as the senior pastor, was in his last year before leaving to become vice-president of the entire Christian & Missionary Alliance denomination. He shared a special bond with Preacher and penned these words:

Philippians 1:3 says, *"I thank my God every time I remember you."*

Remembrances of are built on experiences with. Positive thoughts come from positive interactions and nothing could be more true of my relationship with Preacher Freeland than the words positive and thankful.

I met him several years ago while touring with the Fisherman's Union from Nyack, NY. One of the stops for this fifty-five voice youth choir was Portsmouth, VA, and the Alliance Church. Friendly, warm, personal, sincere, Godly and yet never a hair out of place was my initial memories.

If you never get a second chance to make a first impression then the second encounters with Preacher Freeland have done nothing but re-enforce my first impression of him. Let me share some of these second encounters, three of which summarize the kind of person he is.

When we candidated here in April 1991 Preacher and Mrs. Freeland invited us over to their home. Toward the end of our delicious meal he said, "Dave, if God calls you here I want you to know right now that we intend and promise to be a support and help you in every way we can." I will always cherish what happened in that moment. For what he promised in that private moment he has completely fulfilled. Preacher Freeland has visited, preached, and has graciously and humbly deferred to my leadership even in moments when it was probably difficult. Loving thoughtfulness is my first experience of him.

A second encounter is more than a one-time event. About once every two months in my nearly four-and-a-half years I can hear the doorbell outside the office ring. No one uses the doorbell except Preacher Freeland. So when the office staff hears the ring we know Preacher Freeland is about to ascend the steps to the office complex. When he does he usually slips into my office, asks how things are going, then slaps his hand on my desk and says, "Let's pray." Which is exactly what he does. He prays for me and for the ministry of God through me.

The last memory that stands out in my mind is another cluster of acts. For the last nine months of construction there must be only a few days when Preacher Freeland has failed to make a tour of progress. Day after day I will see him come around the corner of the gymnasium, stroll past the school building and disappear into the new complex. This daily routine communicates his excitement, support, love and desire to see the Alliance Church and Christian school be all it can before God.

Remembrances of are built on experiences with. And I'm sure you'll agree that these memories paint a wonderful picture of Preacher Freeland. God's servant, who is and will always be a man of thoughtfulness, of prayer and of big dreams fulfilled.

Thank you "Preacher Freeland" for first impressions becoming lasting impressions.

— — —

"Retired but not retired" was how Preacher described himself as the months and years rolled by. Not too tired to answer the call when a Sunday School class or small group in the church needed someone to speak. Nor too tired to roam the halls of the Alliance Christian School. It was early 1996 and time for the school to celebrate its 25th anniversary. On a Sunday night in March, a special Alliance Christian School Founders Celebration was held. Not many things happened around Alliance that Preacher didn't know about. But that evening he was taken completely by surprise when, during the program, a sign was unveiled naming the school's gymnasium after him. In addition, it was announced that the new Rev. Earl W. Freeland Gymnasium would be totally refurbished thanks to a contribution in memory of Roy Taylor. Interviewed afterwards by *Virginian-Pilot* sports writer and close friend Bill Leffler, Preacher was humbled to tears. "Seeing my name on that gymnasium isn't something I deserve. There out to be a lot of names on that sign. There were just so many involved. We've come a long way from a basketball net on a light pole."

— — —

After Dr. Gates' retirement in 1995, Clifton Williams was hired as the new school administrator. When this book was originally published in 2000, he was still serving in that capacity. When he learned I was writing **Preacher "*A Man Sent From God,*"** he sent me this letter:

Congratulations on the book you are writing. Reverend Earl Freeland is someone very special in my life. Although I have only known him for five years he has made an impact on me. I feel certain that those who read the book will also be impacted by the life of this faithful servant of the Lord Jesus Christ.

Obviously I would not be serving the Lord where I do if not for the vision of Rev. Freeland. Five years ago when I was asked to serve as the school administrator I found a friend and encourager in Rev. Freeland. He makes regular visits to the school and talks with teachers and students. He also stops by my office and has prayer with me. I know many times he has made these visits when he was in physical pain and yet he took the time and encouraged all of us in the school. He continues to be supportive of the activities of the school and is a great fan of Falcon Athletics. I remember three years ago when he and some others drove several hours to another part of the state to see the basketball team play in the Virginia Independent School state playoffs. His support for the school and the personal support given to me will always be something for which I am grateful.

Alliance Christian School will celebrate thirty years of existence next year and many families, mine included, will again acknowledge the vision of Rev. Freeland. No one knew the impact of Rev. Freeland's faithfulness in starting this school when it began, but many can testify of the impact today.

It will be my pleasure to read the book about this dear man who I am privileged to call a friend. God has truly blessed my life by allowing me to know Rev. Freeland and to be able to serve in this ministry.

Respectfully,
Cliff Williams, Administrator

— — —

The current pastor at the time of the original publication, Rev. Frank Clay, also enjoyed a warm friendship with Preacher. He, too, wanted to include a special tribute:

Always I am aware that the abundant spiritual fruit and blessing these days at the Alliance Church of Portsmouth is largely due to the loving 40-year presence and ministry of Preacher Freeland. After pastoring here 28 years he has remained among us as a wonderful inspiration of servanthood and Godliness. The continuity of Preacher and Mrs. Freeland caring and helping people of one church for many of the people's lifetime is a rare experience in the 21st century. What a delight it is for me to pastor people with such a heritage.

Special are all the services and visits we have shared together since I have come to Portsmouth. Whether communions, weddings or funerals, Preacher is always an example to me in being serious and witty, firm and gentle, down to business and warmly personal, but most of all in the way he shines Jesus. I especially cherish along with others meeting in prayer with this friend of God at dawn on Wednesdays. I can't wait to read this book and get acquainted with my elder brother even better. What a tremendous joy to know Earl Freeland and serve this family of God with him.

Rev. Frank Clay, Senior Pastor

— — —

Well friend, Bud Jr. says it's time we take these memories to the printer. Before we do, Preacher and I want to once more walk the grounds of the Portsmouth Alliance Church. It brings back so many precious memories of Preacher — leaning over the fence at the baseball game; sitting on the porch watching the birds and squirrels; walking into the school gymnasium named after him in 1996; greeting kids in the hallway of the school; standing in the pulpit to proclaim the word of God; just being my friend. I hope you have enjoyed reading about my pastor. There are many tales I didn't include in the book and many more Preacher will make in the years to come. But we'll have to leave them for another time.

[Editor's Note]... As explained in the Editor's Introduction, **Preacher "A Man Sent From God"** was originally published in early 2000. The above paragraph reads exactly as my dad wrote it. It was to be a fitting end to nearly four years of interviews with Preacher, his family and many of those he had loved and influenced throughout his ministry. But the story was not yet complete. In early August 2014, my dad gave me several chapters to add to this book. And, as he's always done with his writing projects, he left it to me to make sense of it all. Not knowing what literary avenue to take, I decided to take Preacher's advice from one of the earlier chapters: "When in doubt, pray about it." The next morning, I remembered something else Pastor Freeland had once said at a Sunday evening service I attended: "I can't save a sinner and neither can you. That's God's department. Our task as Christians is simply to tell people about Jesus and He will do the rest." Talk about an overpowering sense of relief. With that in mind, what follows next is my dad's original **EPILOGUE**, a **NEW EPILOGUE** and then the ending to Preacher's remarkable story. I hope those of you who read the original version more than a decade ago will enjoy this "bonus" section. More importantly, I pray those of you who've made it this far in the book but still haven't made a commitment to Christ will find what Preacher did that night in 1940 at the Fairmont Alliance Church.

EPILOGUE (ORIGINAL)

Passin' it on, he was passin' it on,
From father to son, he was passin' it on.
Passin' it on, he was passin' it on,
Like a bat and a ball, he was passin' it on.
Terry Cashman, from "America's Baseball Heritage in Song"

It's a beautiful Sunday evening in early November 1998. The service at the Portsmouth Alliance Church will not start for another twenty minutes or so, but Preacher is already walking around greeting people as they come into the sanctuary. Freda has already taken her usual seat... middle aisle, 10th row back.

In Bowling Green, OH, Preacher's oldest child, Barbara, is getting ready for church, too. Her husband, Rev. Jim Vandervort, is pastor of an Alliance church there. For a few moments her thoughts turn to Portsmouth, VA, and her dad. She wishes she could see him tonight.

In Clearfield, PA, Preacher's oldest son, Jim Freeland, is also preparing for church. Jim is the song leader at the same Alliance church where Preacher served his last pastorate before coming to Virginia. Jim is a member of the board of governors for the church and teaches a Sunday School class. Just this afternoon he was thinking about his dad and looking forward to when all of the family could be together again.

It is about time for the service to start at the Portsmouth Alliance Church. Preacher's youngest son, Bob, his wife, Kathy, and youngest son, Brian, are sitting a few rows behind Freda. Bob has served the church in many capacities — elder, deacon, board of governors... anywhere he was needed. He and Kathy have also worked many years with the youth of the church, but tonight they're going to sit back and enjoy the service.

The Riverside Quartet from nearby Hampton are guests tonight. The bass singer is Earl Freeland, Jr., Preacher's next-to-youngest son. Earl has been with the quartet since they formed several years ago. The large crowd enjoys the group, as they sing *"To God Be The Glory"* and *"Excuses."* The applauses are loud and the "Amens" are plentiful.

After several numbers, Earl gives his testimony. He tells the congregation how good God is... the God he and his dad serve... a God who never fails. Several months ago he was having physical problems that normal medication didn't help. After exploratory surgery, he was told a cancerous tumor on his lung had spread to his lymph nodes. Through the ups and downs, his faith in God has never wavered. Faith he learned from his dad. During his treatment, he has shared his faith with those he came in contact with — strangers, friends, doctors and nurses. Those who crossed his path heard about the Lord Jesus Christ. Less than one month ago extensive tests were run and although doctors could not explain it, they have declared Earl is cancer free.

"Train a child in the way he should go and when he is old, he will not turn from it." **Proverbs 22:6 (NIV)**

> *Passin' it on, he's been passin' it on,*
> *From father to son and daughter, he's been passin' it on.*
> *He's been passin' it on, to countless thousands,*
> *He's been passin' it on.*

Preacher has passed his love of Jesus to each one of his children — Barbara, Jim, Earl and Bob. He has seen each one of them come to know the Lord as their personal Savior, and baptized and married each of them. Each day of his life, Preacher continues to pass it on — to friend and stranger, alike. May God bless the heritage he is leaving to his family and to so many of us.

NEW EPILOGUE

"Let us not become weary in doing good, for at the proper time we will reap a harvest if we do not give up." **Galatians 6:9 (NIV)**

In 2000, Roots 'n Wings — a small men's group I had started at Alliance — published **Preacher *"A Man Sent From God."*** A total of 300 copies were printed with most of them already pre-sold to church members and friends. On May 20, Roots 'n Wings sponsored a book signing and spaghetti dinner in the fellowship hall that served as a "Celebration of the Life and Times of Rev. Earl W. Freeland." Over 200 people from several states attended the event, many of whom were in tears by the time Preacher's sons, Jim and Earl, had finished the first verse of *"It Took a Miracle."* Preacher was then presented with a proclamation from the City of Portsmouth declaring May 20, 2000, to be Earl Walter Freeland Day; a flag that had flown at the White House in his honor; and a letter of commendation from the mayor of bordering city Chesapeake.

The book was reprinted two more times. After 700 copies, I figured that just about everyone who knew Preacher had one — or at least those folks who wanted to read what I had written. However, as the years went by, I still got calls and emails asking if the book was available. Most if not all shared with me how the book had blessed them or someone they had "loaned" it to. Eventually I ran out of personal copies to give away and in my heart felt I had obeyed the Lord. It was now up to Him to keep it in circulation.

But hold on. In early May 2014 I was at home in deep prayer in my favorite fake-leather recliner when the phone rang. That's not exactly true. The call actually woke me up from my usual afternoon nap. It was my good friend Tal Carey calling from Newport, TN, where he had relocated a few years back. Tal had helped me conduct many of the interviews for the book, including video-taping most of the conversations I had conducted with Preacher. As best as I can remember, Tal said something like this: "Bud, the most amazing thing. A lady in our church was telling everyone about this book someone had given her and what a blessing it had been. I don't know how but she had somehow gotten hold of the 'Preacher' book and couldn't stop talking about it. Between us we've now shared the book with others in the church. The reason I'm calling is to ask your permission to print and sell the book here in Tennessee. The church would like to sell copies to help send the youth on a missions trip."

People still wanted to read it some 14 years later. Wow, I thought. What we're the chances of that. Fortunately I had kept a camera-ready copy of the book so I sent it to Tal the next day. Case closed.

Two days later, again in my recliner and in, um, "deep prayer," I was awakened again. This time it was Alvin Anderson, co-founder of the Alliance Christian School, who I had not talked to since the May 2000 book signing. Alvin said the Lord had been speaking to him about the **Preacher** book and he felt led to try to republish it for God's glory. He believed it could be a means to reaching people with God's goodness and also a way to raise funds for reestablishing the Rev. Earl W. Freeland Scholarship at Alliance Christian School.

A coincidence? Hum.

So I took the idea to my son, Bud Jr., and explained I might need a "little" help. Nothing fancy. Perhaps design a new cover... maybe update the beginning... make a few other small tweaks here and there... and oh yea, add a couple of new chapters to the end. Nothing major, I promised him. I'd like to say he was overjoyed by the opportunity to edit and design another one of my writing projects. Instead, and I've seen this look on his face many times before, he sarcastically said, "Why don't I just edit, rework and rewrite the entire book while I'm at it." Exactly I told him. Aren't sons great.

The three new chapters that follow are my feeble attempt to put a face on the influence Preacher had on my life. They also chronicle several events and happenings that occurred after **Preacher *"A Man Sent From God"*** was first published in 2000.

Chapter 32

Here We Go Again

"There is another who testifies in my favor; and I know that his testimony about me is valid." **John 5:32 (NIV)**

On May 28, 2000, eight days after the book signing, an article by Stephanie Mojica appeared in the *Chesapeake Currents* (a weekly supplement of the *Virginian-Pilot* newspaper) entitled "A Man Sent From God Focuses on Minister's Life." The same article was published a few days later in the *Suffolk Sun*. It read:

— — —

When Earl Freeland was drinking and gambling frequently more than 50 years ago, he never imagined that his life later would be chronicled as an example of God's love.

Freeland, now 84, said he was a "No. 1 sinner" before becoming a Christian at age 24. In 1944, after working in a coal mine for 10 years, he felt called to serve as a minister. Fifteen years later he came to Portsmouth's The Alliance Church, now located on Portsmouth Boulevard.

Bud Key Sr., a church member who lives in the Chuckatuck section of Suffolk, said Freeland's demeanor and the miracles God worked in his life inspired him to write **Preacher *"A Man Sent From God,"*** a book about Freeland's life.

The effort took almost four years, and 300 copies were published. Almost all of them have been sold. The proceeds will go toward establishing an Earl W. Freeland Scholarship. The amount of the annual award has not been determined yet, but the funds will go to help a graduating high school student get a college education, Key said. Freeland served from 1959 to 1997. He is still involved in church activities and helps the current pastor, Frank Clay as needed.

"I'm honored the Lord used me as an instrument to show the miracles performed in Freeland's life," Key said. "It's also nice to reveal how he has helped others through the ministry, and I am proud Preacher and I have been good friends since I came to the church in 1982."

Key said he hopes the book will inspire more people to spend their lives serving God and will offer a look at the daily life of a Christian man.

To celebrate the book's publication and recognize Freeland's accomplishments in the Christian community. May 20 was declared by the city of Portsmouth as Rev. Earl Freeland Day. More than 200 persons attended a spaghetti dinner held at the church.

Another way Freeland has been honored is through Alliance Christian School's gymnasium, which was named after him in 1996. The church established Portsmouth's first Christian high school and the institution now has 300 students from pre-school through high school. Freeland served as interim principal in 1989, 18 years after founding the school. "It is the goodness of the Lord that so many people have been touched through Alliance Church," Freeland said. "Ever since I was saved, I have tried to show God's love. Loving people is the most important thing in the world."

— — —

After the article appeared in the two newspapers, the remaining few copies of **Preacher *"A Man Sent From God"*** quickly sold out. That prompted the Roots n' Wings group to have 200 more copies printed... and then another 200. Although Preacher continued to roam the halls of the Alliance Christian School on a daily basis and faithfully attended nearly every church service, he was now content to watch those he had ministered to and loved for so many years lead Alliance's varied ministries.

Chapter 33

Thanks For The Memories

"Do not let your hearts be troubled. Trust in God; trust also in me. In my Father's house are many rooms; if it were not so, I would have told you. I am going there to prepare a place for you. And if I go and prepare a place for you, I will come back and take you to be with me that you also may be where I am." **John 14:1-3 (NIV)**

I got out of the bed, got dressed, had a cup of coffee, checked the newspaper headlines, fiddled around in the workshop... and then looked down at my watch. It had been 20 minutes since I last checked. With the **Preacher** book "complete," I wondered what I'd do with the rest of my day. For nearly four years I had enjoyed almost daily encounters with the man who for 18 years had been my pastor, mentor, advisor, friend, partner in crime and so many other wonderful influences. I had been a first-hand witness to Preacher in every possible situation and knew that I had been privileged to know a man truly "sent from God." I wasn't the only one worried. I had overheard my wife, Pris, praying (or was it begging?) earlier God would find something to keep me occupied and occasionally out of the house.

Admittedly, I was still busy in the Portsmouth Alliance Church as an elder, chairman of the governing board and member of Roots 'n Wings. But there was a void. So I did what came naturally. I continued to show up on Preacher's doorstep at the parsonage and he continued to invite me in for a cup of coffee and cookies. I continued to shake my head as Mrs. Freeland worked on another jigsaw puzzle. And Preacher and I continued to talk about the goodness of the Lord, often sitting on his porch feeding the squirrels and laughing about our many adventures together.

It wasn't long before a new dynamic was introduced. Tal Carey and Bob Little started showing up, too. Both were members of our Roots 'n Wings group, church leaders, loved Preacher as much as I did, and, well... like me, had nothing better to do. Figuring we all needed a new hobby to keep us out of trouble, Tal, Bob, Preacher and me decided we would take one day a week and visit a town or city not too far away for lunch. It'd be just like the movies *"Thelma and Louise," "Throw Momma from the Train," "National Lampoon's Vacation"* and *"Cannonball Run"* all rolled into one. Maybe not.

For several months in late 2000 and early 2001, Tal, Preacher and me would pile into Bob's car and he would take us to off-the-beaten-path restaurants only he knew about. In truth, a few were quite famous — at least locally. But others were truly roadside "dives" that served some of the best food this side of the Lord's table. Just imagine this gang: an 80-or-something year old retired pastor (Preacher);

a stroke survivor with one leg (Tal); a cancer survivor (Bob) and a somewhat cripple with a metal cage in his back (me). None of us had any trouble falling into Bob's car... it was trying to get out that required weekly miracles. We had some great times laughing, crying and talking about how good the Lord had taken care of us over all the years.

I am convinced the Lord used these weekly road trips to strengthen our faith. In May 2001, Bob Little's cancer resurfaced and less than two months later he went to be with the Lord. I was honored when Bob's wife, Shirley, asked me to give the eulogy at his funeral. I asked God for just the right words. I also asked myself, "What would Preacher say?"

— — —

Tribute to Bob Little
June 19, 2001 • Portsmouth Alliance Christian Church

If you listened real closely early Sunday morning, Father's Day, you could hear a choir of ten thousands of angels as they welcomed Shirley's husband; Kim, Amy and Stephanie's dad; Tara's granddad; and my friend to his heavenly home. Even now that celebration is probably continuing. For you see, Bob Little was a very special man.

Isaiah 40:31 reads: *"They that wait on the Lord shall renew their strength. They shall mount on wings like eagles. They shall run and not be weary. They shall walk and not faint."*

Bob's waiting days are over. He will never again be weary. Nor will there ever be the need to feel faint. Bob will be running through the streets of pure gold and walking through gates of magnificent pearls.

Shirley, Kim, Amy, Stephanie, Tara and the host of Bob's family and friends, know that Bob is completely healed and awaits that day when you will all be together once again.

I met Bob Little several years ago, when he and Shirley started attending our Sunday school class. I could never have imagined the impact that this big quiet man would have on my life. But oh what that impact has been. I am a much better man and Christian for having known Bob these few short years.

As those first months passed by I learned that Bob was a man of extremely high principles, whose word was true. As the months became years I found the priorities that governed his life. First there was his all abiding love of God that always had a way of being the most important thing in his life. Then followed his love for Shirley and his three "little girls." They were truly the "apples of his eye." After these came his love for his church, his love for the "Roots 'n Wings" men's group in the church, his legion of friends, University of Virginia football, cooking and eating.

I watched with great joy as Bob matured as a Christian. He took his talents as a public school administrator into the retirement sector, where he devoted countless hours to serving the Lord and his church. His background in education was a vital asset in his service as a member of the Alliance Christian School board and he was serving as an Elder in the church at the time the Lord called him home.

However it was his untiring efforts in the ministry of Roots 'n Wings that characterized Bob as a true example of practical Christianity. This small group has as a goal to care for one another, learn, and share practical Christianity in their sphere of influence. Bob's life was and is a model I will spend the rest of my life striving for.

It's hard to think of Bob without remembering all those delightful meals he prepared before Wednesday night prayer services. Where did he learn to cook? Who knows; at his mother's knee, out of necessity or "born with it." Whatever, he was the best in the business at it. Bob organized and cooked these meals to encourage more people to attend prayer service and the children's programs. Although they were time consuming, he approached them as an opportunity to serve.

Bob's true Christian character was never more on display than at a 1999 sports breakfast held by Roots 'n Wings for the family of Ken Taylor, football coach for Churchland High School who died after a devastating illness. Bob used his "people skills" to get food vendors to donate more than one thousand dollars worth of food for the meal. He then used his "organizational skills" to see that three hundred attendees at the breakfast were fed a delicious meal in a timely manner. While doing that he spent the entire night before the breakfast in the kitchen preparing and overseeing the preparation of the food.

On a personal note Bob has been a friend who never let me down. He was the brother I never had. Not only did we talk about the Lord but we spent many hours talking about our childhood, our family, Virginia football, Chowan (one of the colleges Bob attended) and Guilford (the college I attended). It's amazing that as we told the same tales over and over Bob's lightning fast tennis serve went from pretty good to over a hundred miles and hour and my batting average soared from the low .240s to well over .350.

And then there were the day trips Bob took me, Preacher Freeland and Tal Carey on. There were many days he would load us up in his car for a destination only he knew; Sunbury, Elizabeth City, Wakefield, Yorktown and on and on. And on each of these trips he would introduce us to some out-of-the-way restaurant that just happened to serve the best food in the county. There was not a town or restaurant in driving distance that Bob didn't know about. And have a story about. The one trip we often talked about was to Roanoke Rapids, NC, to eat at Ralph's BBQ.

The last time I talked to Bob I sat in his bedroom and we laughed about so many things. I reminded him that we still had to visit Ralph's again in Roanoke Rapids. We never got to make that trip. Yesterday morning my wife Pris and I got up and drove to Roanoke Rapids. And we ate at Ralph's. And we talked about Bob. Pris bragged about how she put one over on Bob when he and Shirley were at our home during the Christmas holidays. How she had bought brunswick stew and chicken and rice soup at Bones and Buddy's and how Bob didn't know it wasn't homemade. Well, I have something to tell Pris this afternoon. Bob knew.

Bob's jovial attitude, constant smile and encouraging words have inspired me as a Christian to examine my willingness and my devotion to service for my Lord.

Thanks for your example.

— — —

Although our day trips were now tucked away in my storehouse of fond memories, I continued to visit Preacher as often as possible. On Dec. 4, 2001, I was saddened to learn that Preacher's son, Earl, had been summoned to be part of God's Heavenly choir. Preacher's daughter, Barbara, joined him on Nov. 4, 2003. By the time 2004 rolled around, my wife and I had become the designated link between the church and school at Portsmouth Alliance. We tried everything imaginable to let the teachers and students know how interested the church was in their lives. But the best thing we did was involve Preacher. It was a real treat for the religion classes to have him come in and show the old slides from his missions trip. After captivating the students with many of his experiences, he would always pray for them. You could feel the presence of the Lord as he would finish as he always did with the words, "And I'll thank You. Amen."

In September that year, Pastor Palmer Zerbe asked me if I would conduct one of the Wednesday evening prayer meetings at Alliance. Since Preacher was almost always in attendance, I figured I could convince him to come out of "retirement" one more time and deliver a short sermon before we had testimonies and prayer. How hard could that be? When I approached my friend, he laughed and reminded me Pastor Zerbe had asked me to speak — not him. After a quick pep talk from Preacher (and a reminder he'd be sitting middle aisle, 10th row back), I started preparing a (very) few "words of wisdom" all the while thinking about how he was always able to paint a word picture with his messages. I decided I would do my best to try to emulate Preacher's style. On Wednesday evening, Sept. 8, with sweaty palms, I shared the following with the congregation:

A New Beginning

Picture this scene from the first chapter of Acts. Jesus was in the process of ascending to Heaven from the Mount of Olives. For about 33 years he had lived among them, demonstrating Himself to be the Incarnate Son of God. He had been crucified, had died and had been buried. But, and I have been thrilled on many Easter Sundays as Preacher Freeland painted this picture, He arose on the third day and showed himself by many infallible proofs to be alive.

Acts 1:3: *"After His suffering He showed himself to these men and gave many convincing proofs that He was alive. He appeared to them over a period of forty days and spoke about the kingdom of God."*

He had promised them the gift of the Holy Spirit. He had told them that after receiving this gift, they would be His witnesses in Jerusalem, and in all Judea and Samaria, and to the ends of the earth. And now about 500 of His followers were with him on the Mount of Olives and were watching as He was taken from their very eyes into the clouds. They watched as the resurrected Lord ascended into Heaven.

Wow! Double Wow! Can you imagine the many emotions?

Suddenly, while the 500 or so stared heavenward, two men in white apparel stood by them and asked a Divinely thrilling question: **Acts 1:11:** *"Ye men of Galilee, why stand ye gazing up into Heaven? This same Jesus who is taken up from you into Heaven shall so come in like manner as ye have seen Him go into heaven."*

This question implies and requires action. This is a critical time on God's clock. How these followers respond will forever impact the world. There have been many critical times on God's clock. God has always challenged men and women to stand firm. To do His will.

Noah and the great flood. When you get home tonight read once more the account in *Genesis 6:8-22: "Noah was a righteous man and he walked with God (verse 9). Noah did everything just as God commanded him (verse 22)."* What a task Noah was given. He could have offered many excuses. What would I have done? God, You've got to be kidding. I'm not a veterinarian. Where do I get these animals? I'm certainly not a carpenter. Besides, I don't even know what a boat is.

Then there was Abraham. **Genesis 1:1:** *"Leave your country, your people and your father's household and go to the land I will show you."* I can only imagine what I would have said to God. Man, I'm 75 years old. My bones ache just walking out to the mail box (maybe the well for a drink of water). I've got all my friends here. Who knows what I might find out there. I'm perfectly content here. I'm in my comfort zone.

David and Goliath. We all know the account as recorded in **I Samuel 17**. I'm just a boy, besides the armor doesn't fit. Besides, I'm just the pizza delivery boy.

Elijah as he confronted the 400 prophets of Baal. Joseph, Moses, Daniel, Esther and on and on.

Let's return to the Mount of Olives. The Angels' message is clear-cut, burning into the heart of each person on that mountain. You have a job to do so quit gazing and go do what Jesus told you to do. Forget your disappointments, forget the difficulty, forget the odds. Report for duty at once! Get on with the work he called you to do.

September 8, 2004... a new beginning. Most if not all of us in this prayer meeting this Wednesday night have been in the Portsmouth Alliance Church a long time. We've been on the mountain top and we've been in the deepest valley. We've laughed together and we've cried together. God has a great work for our church. So what are we going to do about it?

Let's look again at Acts. After Jesus' ascension on Mount Olivet and the visit from the two Angels, about 120 of the 500 on Mount Olivet obeyed the Lord and went to the Upper Room to tarry and to pray. Do we really want to see God work in our midst? In our church? Do we want to see men and women, boys and girls accept Jesus Christ as their personal Savior?

I believe that there are four dynamics that need to occur, found in Acts 1 and 2.

First, we need to go to our upper room and tarry. Wait on God for direction. *"Not my will but Thine be done."* Second, we need to pray. Acts tells us they were in the upper room in constant prayer. I'm not talking about "now I lay me down to sleep." We need to get down to business with God. Third, we must be united. **Acts 2:44:** *"All the believers were together and had everything in common. Selling their possessions and goods they gave to anyone as he had need."* Every day they continued to meet together in the temple courts. They broke bread in their homes and ate together with glad and sincere hearts, praising God and enjoying the favor of all the people. And fourth, we must share the good news with those people we come in contact with. Our family, our neighbors, our co-workers, the waitress at the restaurant, everyone. **Acts 1:8:** *"You will be my witnesses in Jerusalem and in all Judea and Samaria and to the ends of the earth."*

God has placed us in our own Jerusalem. Can you be content to stare at the clouds? Doesn't your heart burn within you when to see our church standing as a beacon on Portsmouth Boulevard, inviting all to come to the table and taste His goodness.

Tarry — Pray — Unite — Share. Do what Jesus said.

— — —

I didn't get to speak to Preacher after the service. But secretly in my heart, I hoped he was thinking "I taught him everything I know." I must have done okay because a couple of weeks later Pastor Zerbe asked me to lead the Oct. 6 Wednesday night prayer meeting. That, or he just wanted to give me a second chance to redeem myself. I sincerely wondered if anybody other than Preacher and my wife would show up to hear my ramblings a second time. To my surprise, attendance was even better than before. One old-timer even told me before we began that he kind of liked my style. I resisted the urge to tell him I had learned from the best. Feeling more confident knowing at least one person was in my corner, I spoke that night on the subject "Who is He — Who is that Man?"

I was privileged to speak on several other occasions after that and my wife, Pris, and I continued to write letters of encouragement to the faculty and students at Alliance Christian School. And since I found myself doing something or the other at the church on an almost daily basis, I started visiting with the students and attending a Bible study the teachers had before classes one morning each week — just like Preacher had done for so many years. I was also constantly reminded of Preacher's directive to his congregation: Share Christ with someone else. It seemed like just about every day He would give me a new opportunity to do just that.

At about the same time, God began dealing with me about the lostness of my own family. Starting in early December 2004, Pris and I began spending countless hours locating and inserting ourselves into the lives of relatives I had not seen or even talked to in decades — most who lived in the mountains of North Carolina. With the help of my wife and son, we held a Key reunion in North Wilkesboro, NC, on August 25, 2005. Over 100 family members of all ages, sizes and shapes attended — many who probably came because we had promised them all the chicken and BBQ they could eat. Certain in my heart that many of them didn't know the Lord, I asked my nephew, Randy Carter, pastor of a church in Raleigh, NC, to speak to the gathering. I was also led to print and bring copies of **Preacher *"A Man Sent From God"*** and gave them to those who promised to at least read the first few chapters. I wasn't long before I received phone calls and letters from several of them with the most glorious news in the world — they had accepted Christ as their personal Savior. God was still working miracles through Preacher's example.

Chapter 34

Goodbye, My Friend, Until We Meet In Heaven

"There is a time for everything, and a season for every activity under the heavens."
Ecclesiastes 3:1 (NIV)

It's an interesting phenomenon. As one gets older, time seems to both quicken and slow down. I was 72 years old and seriously wondered how much longer my wife and I would be able to make the 30-minute drive from our home in Chuckatuck (Suffolk) to Portsmouth twice on Sundays and again on Wednesday nights. I was also coming into town on Wednesday mornings to spend much of the day visiting church members with Pastor Zerbe. And, of course, stopping by the parsonage to see Preacher and Mrs. Freeland.

My son, Bud Jr., and his family were now attending Harvest Fellowship — a new church plant in Smithfield — just a few miles away from us and we missed worshipping with them on Sundays. As my wife and I prayed and sought the Lord's will, I thought about Preacher and the tremendous impact he had made not only on my life, but also in the lives of my family and so many others. It occurred to me there was one last mission that needed to be accomplished that would please God and honor my personal friend who meant so much to the Portsmouth Alliance Church. On Feb. 16, 2006, I wrote Pastor Zerbe and requested that the governing board and the elders give serious consideration to naming Rev. Earl Freeland "Pastor Emeritus" of the Portsmouth Alliance Church. I believed it was a long overdue honor.

The motion was approved, and it was decided the title would be bestowed on Oct. 26. However, after several ad hoc committee meetings and talking with Mrs. Freeland, it was decided it would be best to simply bestow the honor without a public celebration. On July 12, without fanfare, the Portsmouth Alliance Church quietly recognized Preacher as its Pastor Emeritus. Less than a month later, a host of angels welcomed Preacher to his new home in Heaven.

A service celebrating the life and ministry of Rev. Earl Walter Freeland, Sr., was held at Portsmouth Alliance Church on the morning of August 14, 2006. Two verses read that day told Preacher's story better than all the words in this book:

"I have fought the good fight, I have finished the race, I have kept the faith. Now there is in store for me the crown of righteousness which the Lord, the righteous Judge, will award me on that day — and not only to me, but to all who have longed

for his appearing." **I Timothy 4:7-8**

""His master replied. Well done, good and faithful servant! You have been faithful with a few things. I will put you in charge of many things. Come and share your master's happiness." **Matthew 25:21**

The service included an organ prelude by Preacher's longtime friend Bernice Verbyla, the song *"It May Be Today"* by the singing mechanic, Chuck Conti, a reading of some of Preacher's favorite passages from the Bible, loving comments by his son-in-law, Rev. James Vandervort, and a closing message by Rev. Palmer L. Zerbe. There was not a dry eye in the sanctuary. After the graveside service, I went home and wept until there were no tears left. I had lost my friend. One part of me was happy that Preacher had been called home, but my selfish side was sad... no porch to sit on and watch the animals stroll by; no fence to lean against and watch the game. It just wouldn't be the same without Preacher.

End of the story? Not quite. A few weeks later, Pastor Zerbe asked me to once again lead the devotions at the Wednesday night prayer meeting. After seeking the Lord's guidance, I knew instinctively what I would say. There was no need to jot down any notes. I simply dusted off an old sermon I had found in a beaten up file cabinet nearly a decade before — one I had heard on Sept. 30, 1984; one with a message that had burned within me ever since; and one so powerful I chose to include in its entirety earlier in this book. That night, fighting back tears, I delivered Preacher's greatest sermon one more time — "Instruments of God." Only this time, I entitled it "A Tribute to Rev. Earl W. Freeland."

On March 19, 2014, Preacher's wife of 73 years, Freda Pauline Freeland, joined him in Glory. They are once again together, only this time, for all of eternity. And that, my friend, is the story of Preacher. As I sit there and finish these last few sentences, I confess I do so with tears running down my face. Memories are like that... they can make you smile and weep simultaneously. Rarely does a day go by that I don't think about my old friend. But it is the assurance that someday soon I will see Preacher again — along with many members of my own family and countless friends like Bob Little who have already gone to be with the Lord — that gives me hope for tomorrow. I look forward to meeting you there, too. All you have to do is accept Christ today into your heart.

EDITOR'S REQUEST

I hope you have enjoyed my dad's heart-felt attempt to share his love of Jesus Christ through **Preacher *"A Man Sent From God."*** If reading this book has made a meaningful impact in your own walk with the Lord, I'm my sure dad would appreciate hearing from you. After all, he now has a lot of free time on his hands... again. The email address is keysknobjr@msn.com.

Also, if you feel led, please help spread the word about the book. In addition to printed copies, **Preacher *"A Man Sent From God"*** is available in ebook format on amazon.com and iTunes. Or, a copy of the book can be downloaded from our website at http://bookbaby.com/book/preacher-"a-man-sent-from-god".

Thank you, again, and may God richly bless you.